I WAS BORN IN AFRICA

A Journey from Motherlessness and Broken Identity

Into Healing and Wholeness

By Vanessa Lawrence

Self-published in partnership with Tell Your Story Coaching

Dedication & Acknowledgment

This book is dedicated to my mother, Maria Fernanda, who did her best to love me in the short time I had her here on this earth, to my late father David, who by default took on the role of both parents to six children under the age of 10, to my beloved siblings, Stephanie, Romayne, Nicole, Nigel, and Ashley, cut from the same cloth but with their own unique story to tell, to the women who helped me during childhood and in my adult life. Some of you will know who you are, others not because you have no idea how a single random act of kindness and compassion profoundly impacted me. To you I say thank you. I would also like to mention my Aunt Wanda, deceased, who stepped in to help the family of her little sister in our time of need. Last but by no means least, this book is dedicated to my own family: my long-suffering husband, Gordon and our children, Harvey, India and Nathan. I love you. Thank you for loving me despite my imperfections as a wife and mother, and finally, this book is dedicated to mothers and daughters everywhere.

I would like to acknowledge Daniella Ordonez. Without my book coach, this book would still be an idea floating in the ether. I am forever grateful for her getting me off the starting line and seeing me to the finish: for her coaching advice, encouragement, prayers, and helping me to begin believing that I have a story which needs to be told.

Preface

Do you have unfulfilled dreams and longings? Have you done what was expected of you rather than followed your passions? Have you made the wrong choices in life and wish you could change your past? Do you feel something is missing in your life; that you aren't truly satisfied or happy? There is always that nagging feeling that there is more to life. Do you feel hemmed in by circumstances and believe that you'll never break out? You have given up expecting a future that will fulfil your dreams, most of which you have probably abandoned years ago. Do you feel like you don't belong but don't know where you fit, or that you are faking it when you are with your peers and that people don't really like you? Have you ever had "imposter syndrome," when you doubt your abilities and feel like a fraud? Are you paralysed by fear of failure? Do you have times of euphoria, then depths of despair, anger, frustration, depression, and hopelessness? Do you just want to discover something new about who you are that will help you find fulfilment in life? I used to say "yes" to all of the above.

I went through cycles of feeling depression, anger, sadness, anxiety, shame, hopelessness, and despair; desiring to break out but always feeling stuck, just like the apple pie bed my older sisters used to make for me as a practical joke. I would be caught out every time as I hopped into bed at bedtime to discover one of the sheets folded back on itself so that my legs could not stretch out; Or when I wanted to be a fast runner. In my imagination, I could run like the wind, but when it came to athletics lessons, I would feel trapped and my body unable to do what I willed it to. I was always being left behind and trailing in at the back. Even my dream life had recurring dreams of being on the run with my brother and sisters from a bad man or monster and I would always get left behind and nearly caught.

This all began to change when one day, in my early thirties, I invited Jesus into my life while breastfeeding my six-week-old daughter. In that peace-filled moment when God took up residence in my heart, I had no idea that He was going to transform my life over the following three decades, nor that I was going to write a book one day. At the beginning of 2023, I began the process of journaling my life story and some of the pain and subsequent healing I had experienced. Upon the discovery that my past can be redeemed, I began to put pen to paper and so began the start of sharing my story.

You don't need to have a relationship with God to read this book, but it comes with a promise that you will encounter Him in the pages and my hope and prayer is that you will be intrigued enough to press on, find out more and make Him your Lord too. It was only through connecting with Jesus and giving Him permission to search and heal my heart that I found real breakthrough. The resolution to my questions, pains and insecurities did not happen overnight but my journey of faith and transformation had begun.

"God, I invite your searching gaze into my heart.
Examine me through and through;
find out everything that may be hidden within me."
Psalms 139:23 TPT

PART ONE: THE JOURNEY

Introduction
LIFE IS A JOURNEY

"Life is a journey not a destination."

Ralph Waldo Emerson

Some people say life is a journey and I tend to look at it that way too, having spent my formative years moving back and forth between West Africa and the United Kingdom. It is true that until we die our lives move forward on a timeline and you may, like me, believe we are eternal, and our spirits live on even after our bodies have worn out.

Our earthly journey is marked by significant events: the first day at school or university, marriage, the birth of a child, a promotion, and so on. The markers might be negative and challenging, such as a season of sickness, the death of a loved one, the breakdown of a relationship. Life has many twists, turns, junctions and crossroads. Sometimes life seems to carry us along as though what happens is out of our hands and sometimes, we have significant choices to make which determine the next stage in our lives. We will always meet people along the way. They can cross our paths fleetingly, leaving little impression, or are hugely influential. Our responses to all that life brings can determine how the next season of our lives pans out.

Jean d'Ormesson, in his poem, "Train of Life," likens our lives to a train ride filled with "joy, sorrow, fantasy, expectations, hellos, goodbyes, and farewells." He writes that the success of our journey depends on how we relate to the people who board our train. Some will stay on; many will step down. We ourselves do not know when it will be our turn to get off and so we must try to live the best way we can by "loving, forgiving, giving and sharing".

Some believe that even at birth we are already marked by the experiences that were going on around us in the womb. Of course, we are strongly influenced by our parents, how they live, where they come from, the culture and times we are born into. The moment we are born we become part of a family. We may be the first child or already have older siblings. From birth, we are always learning and absorbing all that is around us: school, college, work, social life, events, people, and the places we live impact us on the journey.

Chapter 1
MY JOURNEY

Let's start by taking you on some of my life's journey, which even before birth was influenced by my experiences in the womb; my genealogy and the DNA that made up my personality and physical attributes. The path I ended up on was not the path I would have chosen had it been a perfect world. It was one that at times would take me down a dead end, sometimes filled with hopelessness and despair, until I made a change of direction upon accepting Jesus as my Lord and saviour. Since then, He has been my guide, comforter, wisdom and strength, helping me navigate the way forward and re-assess my past through His eyes; which will be shared with you in the forthcoming pages. My desire is that as you read this book, you will find tools and insights that will help you to navigate your own life journey.

By the time I had reached the age of thirty eight, I had moved home so many times that eight years was the longest I'd lived anywhere. That is until my husband Gordon and I, with three young children finally settled in Cornwall, England. Twenty years then hurtled past: the children flew the nest before we knew it, leaving Gordon, me and our bouncy black lab to rattle around in our Cornish home beside the sea, looking forward to longer walks, cycling trips, and more frequent holidays. Perhaps I'd take up an art course or flower arranging; Screech to a halt, let's abruptly stop there-rewind-no thanks! Finding more time on my hands, with Gordon still working part-time, I realised that I didn't want to drift down the route of quietly retiring into oblivion. I realised there was so much more I wanted to do. I'd chosen to give up my career when our first child was born to be a homemaker and mother, which I loved. I was proud of our three children who were a testament to how we'd hopefully raised them, but now I wanted more for my life. I knew that there was more if I could just get hold of it.

However, so many insecurities came flooding in: fear of failure, feelings of inadequacy (I was no longer sufficiently trained in anything) and I was being plagued with bouts of anxiety and low self-esteem which at unexpected times would bombard me and send me into a downward spiral of negativity and defeat. I realised that unmet needs, unhealed hurts and unfulfilled longings were still keeping me stuck in childhood and adolescence causing me to feel paralysed at times throughout adulthood and hopeless about my life. I would occasionally react to people and situations like a petulant child who didn't get her way. In a British TV advertisement for Clarks shoes in the 1970's, five small children stood in a row and in turn told the viewer who they were going to be when they grew up. One was going to be a nurse, another a footballer, and so on. You get the picture. The last little girl looked out of the TV screen and shared a line which was to become immortalised in households, "And according to Mummy, when I grow up, I'm going to be a proper little madam." Suffice to say, that was what I was reminded of every time I stamped my foot, and it has been said that was still occasionally me in my fifties!

I looked back over my life thus far. It wasn't an easy childhood. I was one of six children who lost their mother suddenly when I was five years old, yet muddled through under the care of our able and stoic father and overcame surprisingly well. I left home, went on to university and a short lived career where I met Gordon, and I have been truly blessed with many wonderful experiences and memories for which I am forever grateful. Yet, as my fifties progressed and I was no longer busy in the home, the unresolved issues in my personal life, cycles of despair and hopelessness became glaringly obvious and were affecting my relationships and the decisions I made. I wanted to resolve them once and for all. I wanted to feel fulfilled in my life. Not just for my sake, but for my family and so that I could help others. So I decided to look at my own story, to journal my past and to seek inner healing through Christian ministry and hopefully learn tools to help others.

Our lives are like tapestries: complicated, full, messy, and criss-crossing over into each other's lives and circumstances. As we go through life, we often just stay on the working side of the tapestry where all we see is tangled messes, knots, unfinished stitching and loose threads. If we could just turn the tapestry over to see what our lives have been creating and look from another perspective, we will discover a beautiful work in progress.

So we are convinced that every detail of our lives is continually woven together for good, for we are his lovers who have been called to fulfil his designed purpose. (Romans 8:28 TPT)

In writing this book, I've learned to turn the tapestry over in pursuit of the solution once and for all and have discovered that my life is beautiful poem in the hands of my creator, the master craftsman, and I've found solutions for the bouts of hopelessness, self-condemnation and feelings of failure that were paralysing me from taking action for my future. I had been looking for answers sporadically for some years.

I've always hated what I considered navel gazing and thought it was a sign of weakness to be introspective. My motto was to make the best of life and move on. Yet, I found that I kept repeating the same patterns of being up and down, falling into listlessness, and even despair at times. My emotional life was like a roller coaster which wasn't always easy for my husband, Gordon. For example, I would panic halfway up a steep incline on a bike ride, topple over as fear's icy grip paralysed me from acting rationally. Suddenly, I was no longer able to unclip my cycling shoes from the pedals and more often than not, jammed the chain in the spokes as I tumbled to the ground. Gordon, covered in grease from trying to fix the chain, on one occasion had to cycle home, by now over 10 miles away, and return with the car to rescue me as the chain was damaged beyond repair. I knew I had to find a way to break the cycle of outbursts and overreactions–no pun intended.

Sometimes we have to look back before we can move forward, as there may be things holding us to our past. Maybe we haven't been able to let go and forgive someone, or we were so hurt by an experience that we have shut down in that area and have made an inner vow not to let anyone hurt us or allow ourselves to be so vulnerable again. On the Jewish calendar, the new day always starts at sunset of the previous day. We too want to let the sun go down on our past, to bring closure, so we can begin a fresh new day.

When I decided to earnestly pursue inner healing and began to journal my past experiences, which I found unexpectedly cathartic, to my surprise I discovered that I was beginning to see my past from a different perspective. Although I couldn't undo the events of my life, I could rewrite the narrative. I could choose to react differently and not be a victim of my circumstances. Moreover, I found that there was redemption and love threaded through every season, like gold weaving the tapestry of my life together.

At the same time, I began to value myself. It was subtle at first, the very gentle breath of God as He slowly encouraged me to think more highly of myself and to want good things for my life. This may seem trivial to some, but I bought myself some nice things "just because", I took Gordon on a trip to Thailand with money I'd received from my deceased father's estate. And then in 2023 I began to invest time and money in my future, as I joined an entrepreneur's community, enrolled in book coaching sessions and a heart healing training program. Prior to that, I'd never in my life invested so much in myself! It was liberating.

As I began to find breakthrough, I wanted to be able to share this with others. I learned that to find peace for my soul, I needed to be content with who I am and to know in my heart that I had worth. I discovered that in order to know who I am must begin with experiencing love. From there, long-lost desires and unrealised dreams began to stir and I started to have hope and even excitement for my future, even as I approached sixty! I was beginning to get permission to dream again. As I write this, I still have a way to go, but I'm excited for me and for you, dear reader, as you accompany me on my story.

This book was written for the young me to tell her the things that I had learned along the way; how I found healing and closure of the past and a way to move forward. I wanted to tell my younger self that she was going to be okay and that I understood all of her doubts and fears, her sense of not fitting in and wondering why she felt different. I wanted to tell her the importance of receiving unconditional love, especially the nurturing love of a mother and that when she didn't get it her identity was damaged which led to feelings of abandonment, rejection, anger, depression, isolation, and so much more. I needed her to know that she didn't have to try and be like everyone else and people-please or earn her value through performance and that it is okay to make mistakes, as they don't define who we are. I wanted her to know that she did well in overcoming. That she is a courageous fighter and an overcomer, but that there is also another way to live victoriously by finding her identity. She no longer needed to be in conflict with herself and the world. I wanted to give her tools to help her move forward. I also wanted to help those who had reached a certain age who felt that it was too late to live again, to have renewed hope, expectancy, and peace in their hearts, by speaking to the young girl in them. This book was born from a need to break out of over fifty years of not living my life to the full into one of freedom, joy, and hope.

> ***"Arise, shine, for your light has come and the glory of the Lord rises upon you."***
>
> ***(Isaiah 60:1, ESV)***

My desire is that this book will speak to the young girl in you, too. Whether you are a teenager or already in your autumn years, helping you to redefine your identity, purpose and where you fit in your world so that you are better equipped to make the right decisions, choose which paths to take and how to negotiate the next leg of your journey.

Chapter 2
PRINCESSES, CASTLES, AND HAPPY ENDINGS

And they all lived happily ever after.

Children all over the world have loved fairy tales for their ability to transform them into magical fantasy realms where battles ensue between good and evil, and good wins as the hero, often a handsome prince, rescues his beautiful princess and *they all lived happily ever after.* Snow White, Cinderella, Rapunzel and Sleeping Beauty are all such tales where true love rescues and prevails. In each story, the princess does not know her true identity until she meets her handsome prince, and she is awakened within and transformed as he expresses his love for her and his commitment to be with her forever.

Across generations, little girls have loved to dress up as princesses, longing to escape into a fantasy world where they are rescued by a handsome prince to live long and happy lives together.

Romantic films move us all. Happy endings are always great tear-jerkers, often releasing surprisingly deep wells of unspent emotion. What depths of sadness and sorrow when in the story the love is unrequited, or the couple end up parting. We cry inconsolably and can't understand why we are so moved to tears. Even my husband cries when the family dog dies in *Marley and Me* or when Joey in *Warhorse* is reunited with his owner!

Take Cinderella, her mother dies when she is very young, and her well-meaning father remarries. Cinderella gains an abusive stepmother and two cruel stepsisters. She is known as Cinderella as she spends her days cleaning and raking the ashes in the grates of the fireplace. Cinderella goes about her day singing and uncomplaining. She tries her best to be thankful, to honour her father and make her new family happy. She only succeeds in fuelling their hatred and anger. This culminates when she is chosen to be the bride to the prince in the kingdom. Her family is incredulous that of all the handmaidens in the kingdom, he chooses her. All they see is a young, dirty servant girl and are incensed with jealousy and hatred. The prince sees her true beauty: full of grace. Because of her sweet nature, Cinderella can forgive her ugly sisters and even arranges marriages to noblemen for them. Apart from being a beautiful story of redemption where love wins, it is a lesson in kindness, forgiveness, graciousness, and reconciliation.

Another of the most well-loved fairy tales of all time is *Sleeping Beauty*. Even though it's a magical tale filled with fantasies, fairies and spells it tells the real story many of us are living today of unfulfilled lives which are sabotaged from the womb, attacking our identity, BUT the good news is that it doesn't have to stay that way. This book will break the spell that keeps us inert and asleep in thinking there is nothing we can do to change our own circumstances. It will help us awaken to the truth of who we are and invite us to rewrite our own narrative to give a happy ending.

Let's look at the story in a little more depth. In an unnamed European kingdom, the king and queen are holding a great party to celebrate the birth of their daughter, Princess Aurora. The couple have waited a long time to have a baby, and they want to make this celebration as lavish as possible. They invite many important guests, including a group of good fairies who are to be Princess Aurora's godmothers. Each fairy is invited to give the princess a special gift, such as beauty or a song to protect her throughout her life.

However, one fairy, Maleficent, has accidentally been overlooked and hasn't been invited to the party. She bursts in unannounced, in a terrible rage about the oversight. She approaches the baby's crib and places a curse on her. She says that before sunset on her sixteenth birthday, Princess Aurora will prick her finger on a spindle and die. Maleficent then makes her exit, leaving the rest of the guests shocked and devastated.

One of the good fairies hasn't yet given her gift to the baby princess. She attempts to undo Maleficent's curse so that instead of dying, the princess will fall into a deep sleep that will last for one hundred years. She will only wake when a prince kisses her with true love.

To protect the princess, the king orders every spinning wheel and spindle in the whole kingdom to be destroyed. Princess Aurora is sent into the woods to live with the good fairies until she is sixteen.

We next meet the princess on her sixteenth birthday. She doesn't know she is a princess, as she only remembers being brought up in the forest by the fairies. However, that night there is to be a party at the castle to celebrate the princess's birthday. The fairies tell her of her true identity.

When Aurora arrives at the castle, she meets an old woman, who lures her away into an isolated tower. The old woman is Maleficent in disguise, and she has a spinning wheel with a cursed spindle. Aurora touches the spindle and pricks her finger. Instantly, she falls into a deep sleep.

The good fairies see with horror what has happened. They place the sleeping Aurora on an ornate bed in the highest tower of the castle. Then, realising that by the time she wakes up, everyone she has known will be gone, they magically send everyone in the castle into the same deep sleep. All the inhabitants of the castle will only wake at the same time as Aurora if she is kissed by a prince. The fairies make the trees and plants of the forest grow into a tangled web that completely covers the castle so nobody can disturb Aurora's sleep.

One hundred years later, a handsome prince is riding his horse through the forest. He sees a huge tangle of brambles and realises there is a castle hidden beneath it. Filled with curiosity and wanting to explore, the prince cuts his way through the web of brambles and enters the castle. Once inside, he climbs the stairs until he reaches the very top of the tallest tower, where the princess lies asleep.

When the prince sees the sleeping Aurora, he instantly falls in love with her. He approaches her and gives her true love's kiss. At this moment, Aurora and all the castle's other inhabitants wake up. The prince and princess are married, and everyone lives happily ever after.

Even though the story of *Sleeping Beauty* is a fantasy, one of its appeals, like all fairytales, is that we long to identify with the hero or heroine. In an ideal world, we would all be born to well-off, influential, loving parents who want us and who love us unconditionally. First, through the nurturing and care of our mother and then through our father who stretches us and helps us grow and step into our identity in a safe environment. Think of your one-year-old child. The umbilical cord is cut, the baby is laid on the mum's breast who is now responsible for breastfeeding, weaning, and cuddling. Some months later it is Dad who throws her up in the air, bringing excitement and fun. His arms are ready to catch her as she squeals in delight while Mum looks on anxiously in case Dad misses the catch. I know this is stereotyping but you get the idea. Our parents meet our needs, protect us and help us grow and discover our gifts and talents which we develop in a safe environment. We are born with innate gifts and skills, which, in perfect circumstances are nurtured and developed and we blossom into the unique personality we are created to be.

The world is not perfect and most likely our experience is not that of a privileged princess born and raised in a palace with every need met or a hero to the rescue. We innocently tumble into the world where the odds may be stacked against us already. The name Maleficent means to cause harm or destruction and so often our lives get sabotaged very early on and we lose sight of who we are and our unique calling and identity.

Like Aurora, whose name means Dawn, and who was awakened with a kiss, I want to help you wake up to your identity and why you need to know who you are. You may not even realise that you're not being the real you or all you can be. You may have just accepted the status quo, or perhaps you have always felt dissatisfied, not at ease with who you are, or don't even like yourself. You know there is more to your life, but you can't seem to find it. I want to tell you that it is only waiting for you to discover. You can be redeemed from a life that seems cursed. You can be awakened to find out who you were designed to be and you *can* live happily ever after.

It is also my hope that this book will help you get off the treadmill of performance and people-pleasing to earn love and acceptance so that you can be free to be all you were meant to be. There is a unique plan for your life that only you can accomplish. We all have hopes and dreams, but we can't find our true purpose, which is the only way we will be fulfilled until we know who we are.

In the next section of this book, I will share my story in the form of journaling that I would want my younger self to read to help her make sense of her early years. This will include how I interpreted my experiences, the ups and downs, and the struggles and challenges I faced for years.

This will be followed by lessons I've learned, the wisdom I've gained and the conclusions I've come to. We will look at the definition and importance of identity, and how unconditional love at an early age is a crucial factor in finding identity, with an emphasis on the nurturing love of mothers in our formative years (ages 0-8).

Weaved throughout I will share parts of my own story to show how our identity can become attacked, distorted, and impaired. This will help you understand some of the causes and symptoms of having a broken identity.

I will give the tools I have learned on restoring and living out identity, how to move forward in one's purpose and which actions can be taken to find healing and wholeness with practical applications. These are by no means inexhaustible. I do not claim to have found all the answers. These are simply my observations from my personal experiences which I hope will stir you to look at your life, even as you question and may not agree with all that is written.

Chapter 3
JOURNALLING MY LIFE

Formative Years

I was born in Nigeria, West Africa in 1964. I am number five of six children. The youngest, a sister, Ashley with a mop of Shirley Temple curls and a cute smile that even melted the hearts of grown men, arrived four years later and stole the show. So she should have, my adorable little sis.

My father, David, an ex-army officer, had taken my mother and three daughters to live in the capital, Lagos in his new civilian role as manager for Nigerian Breweries Ltd. My brother, Nigel, a boy at last (which is possibly why, hoping for another, they had intended to name me Paul) and then I and Ashley were born in fairly quick succession. My poor mother had six children under the age of ten in tow. She was Portuguese-Catholic, born and raised in the Portuguese colony of Macau and then Hongkong, where she met her dashing, uniformed husband, and father of six-to-be, David, a war child and the youngest of five. David's stay-at-home father was not considered well enough to fight, his mother ran the household, rationed the food, and scolded the children as needed. On one occasion she chased him around the garden with a shoehorn after he had opened the oven door and ruined the angel cake which she had spent weeks saving up the ingredients for during the rationing of wartime Britain. Air raid shelter in the garden and close enough to London to hear the bombs, David and his brother spent hours playing with sticks for guns and stones for bombs. At the age of fourteen, he packed his bag and joined the army, training to be an officer at Sandhurst Royal Military Academy. He spent time in Egypt as a cartographer before being posted to Hongkong to be part of the Gurkha regiment, where he fell in love on a tennis court with my mother, the little sister of a friend. Three months later they were married. Married life must have come as a shock to both. Sex before marriage was strictly taboo and living together before your wedding day was unheard of. Then, moving to a foreign land, Africa at that, away from her large close-knit family, with poor communications, must have been difficult and lonely for my mother. Having lost her own mother around the birth of their second child, Romayne, and probably longing for airmail letters from siblings and friends which could take weeks to arrive, would have been a lonely and isolating experience. Bearing six children in quick succession created an even greater strain although it certainly kept her busy with little time to be homesick.

No doubt, family life was hectic and that is probably why one of my earliest memories (or maybe I was told this later) was of crawling around on the floor while the family piled into the car, travelling several miles before noticing I wasn't with them. Perhaps this was the start of an unspoken inner sense of abandonment.

Later, when about three or four years old and not so easy to be forgotten, my position in the car as the smallest was to stand on the hump in the floor between the back seats and hold on for dear life to the front seat headrests. Not having car indicators in those days, my parents would stick their arms out of the window at every turn, a dangerous endeavour in the roaring, horn honking, and dusty traffic of Lagos where your arm could be chopped off by robbers wanting your watch. From my precarious position, I often remember circling a roundabout piled high with abandoned rusty and broken-down cars on our way to church on Sundays. My mother, veil covering her hair, sitting composed in the front, her one attempt at serenity in her week of child rearing oblivious to the jostling and arguing of five children in the back seat of our Vauxhall Cortina. The dirt and hubbub of the streets filled with hawkers, beggars and mamas carrying their babies on their backs, trays selling their meagre wares balanced on their heads as they swayed gracefully along the sidewalks. The sights and sounds of this gritty metropolis are forever etched in my memory.

Over half a century later, as I tried to gather snapshots of my mother from the recesses of my mind, a memory made and seemingly lost in the womb barged into the light of day with such ferocity that it stopped me in my tracks. The memory was of my mother pregnant with me, crying out in anguish and exhaustion to my father "I don't want another baby." Who knew? I can't go and ask my father if this actually happened as he died just before the start of Covid. He made it out before lockdown and the onset of dementia could shut him down completely at the grand old age of eighty-six. It would help explain the nagging feeling I have dragged around with me my whole life that I'm not really wanted or needed; that I don't add value to the party. Truth be told that I'm not really liked. That's the narrative playing in my head so often. Can't someone just turn over the record?

My mother, Maria Fernanda de Menezes Rodrigues (Dad used to roll her name off his tongue to our delight when we would pester him to tell us about her), to be immortalised as Mummy, was snatched from us far too young. Sitting in the front passenger seat, composed, hands in her lap, lace head scarf over her head, beautiful, petite, studious, gentle, quiet mummy who loved to expand her vocabulary by reading the dictionary. She could converse in up to nine languages: being fluent in Portuguese, Chinese, English, and French. A fact I proudly shared and one of the memories I had accumulated in my meagre storehouse of recollections: Mummy, Nana, ballet dancer, wren, nurse, wife, sister, youngest daughter of nine children taking her family to church. I loved knowing who she was.

Moving from Nigeria was a bit of a blur, other than my father was switching roles as manager of Nigerian Breweries Ltd. to that of Ghana Breweries Ltd. My sisters were packed off to boarding school in England leaving us three younger ones at home.

I usually hasten past that dark time in Ghana, it's always been rushed through and although not said as such, has been *let's move on, everything is fine*, hovering over our family like an embarrassment that no one wanted to discuss too deeply or share with others. Perhaps they would cringe and be awkward and it would hang in the air causing discomfort. It wasn't what happened to normal people–right? So, why mention it? It was to be looked at only in passing, not dissected, or dwelt on. Don't make things uncomfortable. My father was from a fatherless war time generation. A British one at that: with a stiff upper lip, no need to show your emotions, *move on, old chap*. In fact, I've always remembered one of Dad's favourite words was *fine*, a word I came to hate. If ever I asked him his opinion, be it over an outfit I was planning on wearing, a job I was considering taking, a meal one of us had spent hours labouring over in the kitchen (we girls all learned to cook at a young age) it was always...fine. Nothing more and nothing less. It plastered over the deep seat of unhealed hurts, unspoken pain and broken dreams.

Mummy's Demise

So, I will share the little I know of Mummy's death. My sisters were at boarding school, my brother and I in our shared bedroom when my father woke us in the middle of the night, speaking in hushed tones so as not to wake the baby. I have something to tell you, he said, as he sat on the edge of my bed. Hovering outside, an elderly couple, Edna and Claud, waiting to offer loving support. Edna used to exercise by bending down, her legs as straight as possible to reach a box of Swan matches, picking one up at a time and putting it on a high shelf until she or the box were exhausted.

I don't remember what my father shared then or what I found out later, but this is what I know: they had been to a party, he and our mother. She didn't drink. Whenever I subsequently tell people, I always feel I have to tell them that as if I need to defend her character. My mother wasn't a drinker, I say.

She choked and began to vomit, but not wanting to cause a scene or attract attention, she tried to swallow her own vomit and suffocated. No one was able to help. Dead by the time the ambulance came. *Boom*–she was alive and now is dead. My father, now newly labelled widower.

We were considered too young to attend the funeral, but we saw a couple of Polaroid photographs of a gravestone with flowers. Those pictures eventually faded and became blurred like the memory of our mother. My brother and I sat up in bed and cried on receiving the news, but at the tender age of five, I didn't really understand the implications of the loss. All I remember was that I stopped crying very quickly until seeing my brother continue to sob. I thought, I'd better cry some more. I think that may have been the start of a hardening of my heart. By the time I was an adult I rarely cried and thought it was a weakness in others. Although, there would be times when those old wounds would be prodded, poked, opened, and unexplainable tears would flow like the torrential rains of Africa and then stop as abruptly as they'd begun. I'd be spent and like the rains that had drained away so quickly I couldn't grasp or understand why I had reacted with such grief to perhaps a boyfriend breaking up with me or a soppy romantic film. This was in contrast to the times when I'd feel absolutely nothing. I'd be no good as one of those official grievers at funerals. Give me a death any time, even a family one, and you'd rarely see tears. Lip service maybe but rarely tears. On one occasion I was forgotten by a friend's mum who was supposed to pick me up from my grandmother's house and take me to an eighth birthday party. I'd actually been invited to a party! That was unusual when you didn't have a mum who was part of the school gate circuit where coffee mornings were arranged, children's social lives and school clubs were planned, gossip banded about planting seeds of destruction as lives were dissected. I sat on the bottom rung of stairs in the narrow hallway of her Victorian semi, waiting with anticipation and trepidation, ears straining for the sound of a car pulling up, which never came–she'd forgotten. My hope and expectation turned into doubt, into why hasn't she come? What's wrong with me? To acceptance and then numbness. Such a simple, understandable mistake that would be forever etched in a child's memory.

Life after Mummy

So what was Dad to do with no wife or mother to his three children under the age of seven, let alone three in boarding school? The decision was made that we would return to the United Kingdom. Ashley was to stay with an aunt in England while Nigel and I were whisked off to boarding school. Nigel was to join his older male cousin and I to be with my sisters at their convent. The school took in children from the age of seven but the headmistress, nicknamed Fish by the girls, owing to her rather large mouth and which I was the only one who got away with saying to her face. It's amazing what you can get away with when you're young, cute and have just lost your mother. She made an exception to the rule by allowing me to board there while Dad worked out what to do next. I stayed a year, during which time I'm told I was incredibly spoiled by the older girls, which my family used as an excuse to knock out of me in the holidays, not literally I hasten to add.

It wasn't too bad at boarding school. After all, I was doted on by the "big girls," although my one abiding memory was of locking myself in the art cupboard having swallowed some dye which I'd got on my fingers and not allowing anyone in as I thought I was about to die. Fear of death had managed to move in without much opposition. After some coaxing and promises of an extra-large portion of dessert that evening I emerged unscathed and ravenous. The fear of death could wait.

Years later, I am sharing this incident at a women's prayer conference, describing the sense of panic that I had no mother to help me, moreover that I had lost her at such a tender age. Sobs break out in the room as other women, some of whom lost their mother's decades earlier, release their grief for the first time.

Adjusting to Life Back in Africa

Dad soon moved with Ashley and me back to Nigeria where he could continue to pursue his career and the others joined us during their school holidays. Thankfully Dad had consulted us kids over whether Ashley should stay with our aunt who was willing to adopt her or live with us and we unanimously chimed that we wanted to stay together at all costs. We couldn't face another loss and the bond between us was fierce.

Life actually became quite normal. Children get on with their lives. School in the mornings, freedom to play in the afternoons which sometimes involved going down to the creek, a dark swamp teeming with life and eerie sounds. Flashbacks of Africa evoke longing and belonging even today.

I would often be found (if looked for) playing in the dirt of the compound with the children of our Nigerian cook, Peter, whose large and ever growing family lived in a home in our backyard; or chatting to the watchman who sat under the shade of a huge tree at the front gate where our resident monkey made his home in the branches.

One time I returned home with a jar of tadpoles which Peter allowed me to put in an open glass tank in the kitchen. Why on earth we had a tank eludes me to this day. Every day I peered through the glass until one by one their legs and arms developed, their tails dropped off and we came down one morning to frogs hopping all over the kitchen counter. Needless to say, that was the last time I was allowed to bring wildlife into the house, but not the last time I was given freedom to do things. Being allowed to pursue my own adventures while my siblings were back in England was actually quite a lonely time for me. It compacted the belief that I had to handle life on my own and I became quite adept at it. Ashley, meanwhile, spent most of her time in the not so capable hands of the nanny my father had brought with us from the United Kingdom.

Life Back in Africa Cut Short

A few months later, we returned by ship to the United Kingdom for a holiday and I had free run of all three decks. No one seemed to notice where I was, so I found myself watching the adult rated horror movie every day that was screened on repeat in the ship's auditorium, or wandering about in third class where I encountered a lone family who couldn't afford to join the well-off masses. I wondered; did they feel as alone as I did?

When the others were home from boarding school, Saturdays were spent at the open-air pool of the Federal Palace Hotel with other families and on Sundays we took a banana boat over to Tarqua bay, an endless stretch of sand from where you could see across to an island which housed a high security prison. Our imaginations ran wild.

More than once, we spent the night in huts along the tree line by the beach, raised on stilts to keep the predators away, and woke with the dawn to watch the local fishermen bring in their haul of sprats which were fried and we ate for breakfast, crispy and delicious. One memory that weighs heavily on my mind even today was the sound of cries coming from another family's hut and feeling scared but helpless as my older sister explained in hushed tones that our friend was being beaten by her father. Why did no one say anything? Why didn't the other adults help? This compounded my belief that children had to learn to cope and look after themselves.

In general, life was okay. No, it was good, especially when we were all together during the holidays. My best times were when "the others" as Ashley, Dad and I referred to our siblings, came home for the holidays. The house was full of activity, laughter, and family games. Stephanie, being the eldest, was in charge, Romayne, the second-in-command, followed by Nicky, a mischievous Nigel, me and lastly adorable Ashley.

We would enjoy endless hours playing 52-Scatter, Kick-the-Can, Sardines, and murder mysteries. It was so much fun when we were together despite the occasional hair pulling, catapult shots from Nigel's catapult and the snapping of wrists on the latest fad called clackers– two balls on two pieces of six inch-length string knotted together at the top which you held in your hand and shook up and down in hope that the balls would swing up together to clack at the top and then swing down and clack at the bottom in endless rhythm. Truth is, I never once got the hang of it and was quite glad when they were banned as dangerous following many broken wrists. I also never got the hang of Racing Demon, a fast and furious card game which the older ones always won and which left me furious and determined to win at something. Of course, it is normal in families for the older, stronger, and more knowledgeable ones to dominate, but I would end up feeling helpless and powerless. That was another lie I told myself, to add to my arsenal.

Instead, I took it out on Ashley. Dad used to give us weekly sweets and I would hide mine behind my back and then sweetly tell her that I'd run out and would she share? Wide eyed and innocent Ashley obligingly gave me half of hers and then with glee I would produce mine and wolf them down in front of her. Of course, Dad cottoned on and began buying Ashley sweets he knew I didn't like.

It may sound strange, grand, colonial, and definitely offensive to our modern minds, that we had a cook in Africa. In 1960s Nigeria, many Westerners had a day and night watchman to protect their home, a cook and a "small boy "who did household tasks. In actuality, our small boy, Abadu was a handsome regal young man. He was a prince from a local tribe who I remember some years later, when no longer working in our home, sought refuge as he was being hotly pursued by another tribe. My father, duly hiding him and sending away the machete wielding aggressors until danger had passed. Peter ran the household and did the cooking. Chicken with rice and peas were my favourite but he was famous for his curry with accompaniments and my father would proudly loan him out to other households like a prized trophy. As I write this now, in the twenty-first century, I'm actually horrified at how archaic and politically incorrect our lives were back then. As a child, I accepted it and knew nothing else. In fact, to me they were like a surrogate family and even though their lives were so different, I longed to be part of the hustle and bustle of normal family life.

I even cultivated a Nigerian accent which I could turn on and off at will, a questionable skill which I would produce with relish in my later childhood in England, which amused only me. I recall as a teenager travelling by train to London and spotting a Nigerian man at the far end of the carriage (another of my unusual skills was that I could spot a Nigerian anywhere) and going up to him, I paraded my accent proudly as I made small talk. I discovered as I grew up that I was prone to impetuousness, sometimes throwing myself into life with no thought of the dangers and risks. I look back and think there must have been an unseen shield of protection as I consider how I actually made it through mostly unscathed, getting in and out of scrapes but avoiding major hurdles and pitfalls. I wonder if it was because of my mother's prayers. She was no longer with us, but maybe her supplications had reached out into our future lives, like unseen tentacles wrapping around us, nurturing, and watching over.

One thing I loved to do, until my father was horrified to discover, was learning how to clamber up the side of our water tank behind the house which collected rain water in the wet season. I would sit precariously on its thin metal lip before hurling myself into the stagnant, tepid water on those long hot oppressive days when we were longing for rain. When the rain came, the heavens opened and torrents fell and we children would hastily change into our swimsuits and rush outside, laughing and running about in the downpour. As instantly as it came it was gone again and the water would drain away as though it had never been. Except for that water tank which would be replenished and afford me those infrequent moments of delicious joy. I'm not sure, to this day, if Dad was aghast because of the danger I'd placed myself in or because of my polluting our water system.

I wonder now if my escapades, although not wildly rebellious or daring, were my cry for someone, anyone, to put in boundaries that my mother would have given me.

In the winter of 1970, Dad, Ashley, and I spent two weeks travelling by ship to the United Kingdom to spend Christmas with his mum, who we called Nana (not to be confused with my mother, Maria Fernanda, also known as

Nana) and to see the rest of our siblings. Nigel was still ensconced in boarding school to make things easier for Dad. It was hard for a seven-year-old to be abruptly snatched from both parents at such a tender age but was a relic of the Victorian age when children born into comfortable homes often had nannies, rarely seeing their parents throughout the day. Being whisked off to boarding school as young as five was the norm. Boys especially were expected to grow up and act like a man, which meant not showing their feelings, and to cry in public was unacceptable. They should be seen and not heard. Of course, we weren't like that, but the best solution under the circumstances was to send Nigel away when he needed a mother the most.

The plan was to spend the Christmas holidays with Nana and then return to Lagos but due to escalating civil unrest in Nigeria, Dad reluctantly decided it wasn't safe for us to return to Africa. That Winter, we all went down with chicken pox and I spent Christmas day in bed. When finally better, I got up to discover my present, a miniature kitchen with actual fire lighters that could heat up water on the little stove, had been ripped into and used by my siblings.

That's family life when you're one of six and where the older children take on parental roles. Life without a mother was beginning to impact me as I no longer had the security of her protection. I was starting to realise that I was the only one who was going to fight my corner.

Every time we moved across continents, our belongings had to be shipped and I remember Dad leaving behind the few toys and books we possessed in

Nigeria as he thought we would return, but never did. A sense of temporariness, not belonging, looking to lay down roots but not able to find anything to put them into began to frame my life. Regarding relationships, especially with mother figures, I was always grasping for longevity but people flitted in and out, never staying for long. There was the beautiful and kind air hostess who Dad dated and who brought me a mango from one of her travels and the Dutch mother who tried to include me in her daughter's birthday party, but who forgot to give the instructions in English. All of the children ran off to play the game, leaving me standing, not knowing what to do, and awkwardly sticking out like a sore thumb again. I didn't enjoy the wrong kind of attention! Then there were the various nannies and babysitters who Dad needed to employ to look after us after school.

My sisters and brother returned to boarding school and my stint with Nana lengthened into a year. She looked after Ashley and me while Dad travelled for work in the United Kingdom. Perhaps living with Nana would bring some stability into my life, although this was not to last either.

We settled into a routine of daily walking to and from the local Catholic school on our own. Memories of nuns in habits, imagination running wild about bloomers underneath their robes (I remember once seeing a humongous pair drying on the radiator in sister's office), and in all that time I gleaned several things: that I had a guardian angel apparently, that God was sitting on His throne somewhere in heaven from where He ruled the universe, ready to tut-tut, point His finger at me and tell me off. I also believed that by reciting the only prayer I knew at bedtime about pots and pans, saints and doing things in the kitchen, that I could get off to sleep more quickly. I learned to never wear new patent leather shoes to church. On my first Holy communion, I had to walk to the front in my new white dress and shiny white buckled shoes. I looked like the picture of innocence but felt very self-conscious and anxious; even more so when I skidded on the slippery polished floor and fell over. Everyone gasped and rushed to help me, except Nigel, who, nodding off because of boredom and heat eventually keeled over, hitting his head on the pew.

Children are not consciously cognisant of the safety and comfort their mothers give them, but when it is absent, it causes anxiety, stress, and uncertainty about whether anyone will be there for them. I look back and I realise I lived a lot of my childhood in such a state, fearful of being exposed to situations that I could not handle on my own.

But we behaved gently when we were among you, like a devoted mother tenderly caring for her own children. (1Thess. 2:7 AMP)

Much of our time was spent playing by ourselves at Nana's. I doubt her house had been decorated since the war and contained old relics, including Nana herself or so it seemed to a seven-year-old child. Nana led a simple, frugal post-war life and expected us to fit into her routine and habits. Top and tail wash every day except on Saturdays when we had a lukewarm bath in only a few inches of water in an iron bath in the freezing bathroom. Bed by 7 pm except on Wednesdays when I was allowed to stay up to watch TV until 8 pm. Turfed out into the garden to play after meal times, rain or shine on Saturdays and Sundays. Up early to bring her a cup of tea in bed at 7 am on the weekends. A two mile hike alone (again) to and from church on Sundays.

Early Faith Experiences

I didn't really have much faith then, although every night I said my prayers: God bless Daddy, God bless Stephanie, Romayne, Nicole, Nigel, until I got to Ashley and eyes heavy with sleep would drift off into occasional dreams of being chased by boogie men and always getting left behind as my faster, older siblings ran off. My way of escape was to jump into a body of water which would wake me up–phew, safe again!

I was becoming intrigued by Nana, who was, as she called herself, a spiritual healer. People would come to the house and they would go to the "back room," a dark and musty sitting room with heavily draped windows, where she would call up spirits of deceased loved ones and record the sessions on an ancient tape recorder.. I would press my ear against the door straining to catch these encounters between the earthly and spiritual realms. This set me on a path searching for spiritual experiences. As kids we would try to call up Mummy using ouija boards. We practised levitation, white magic and read tarot cards. You name it, we tried it. It all seemed harmless and it was motivated by an inner longing to connect with the spiritual world, where we might just somehow be able to connect with Mummy.

It was Mummy's faith that ended up being the greatest influence on my spiritual journey. I was first exposed to the liturgy of the Catholic Church from birth, attending mass on Sundays until my mother's demise. Later, when living at Nana's, Dad enrolled me in the local convent school. He'd stopped attending church. He probably couldn't face all things "mummy" and more likely was questioning his own faith but had obviously decided that didn't exempt me and that I should go. What happened to practise what you preach? Mass on Tuesdays in the school chapel and church on Sundays. I would be sent on my own to walk the two miles there and back. It was quite handy actually as Nana would give me fish paste sandwiches for lunch, which I hated, so, every time I made the walk to church or school, I would drop them conveniently into the rubbish bin of a house we passed. This was extremely handy until one day the bin was no longer at the end of the drive. Horror and panic overwhelmed me, what was I to do?

The next plan quickly bubbled to the surface, it seemed such a good idea and so I began to carefully prop my sandwiches against the base of Nana's rose bushes in the back garden. Nana loved her roses, as did I, tending them regularly and planting new ones when a close friend or relative died. So, of course it wasn't long before she discovered little packs of sandwiches strewn around the garden like fertiliser flung from an unseen hand. Having raised children through World War Two, where there were severe shortages, rationing, and "waste not, want not," was the saying of the day, you can imagine that discovering several packed lunches didn't go down well with Nana. How naïve I was to think I wouldn't be caught and scolded. So this demanded some serious planning for future sandwich disposal. Nana had a tall free-standing cupboard in her spare bedroom. In summer, it housed a sumptuous feather eiderdown, a perfect place to hide a sandwich deep in its folds. That is until Nana pulled it out when the winter months drew close to discover a ruined mouldy eiderdown. By then we were living elsewhere and I distinctly recall Dad receiving the phone call. As he tried to placate her, we could hear Nana's raised voice down the phone. We didn't know what had happened yet but knew someone was in trouble. Please don't let it be me! Too late and it added to the growing fear of not wanting to be chastised but always seeming to do the wrong thing, which would pile on the shame and blame. Later I would (and still do) have a tendency to shift the blame whenever someone does something wrong. "It wasn't me," I exclaim, or "But you said...!"

Nana (pronounced *a* for apple and not to be confused with open your mouths and say *aah* for Nana, christened Fernanda), as I mentioned, was a spiritual healer. She looked like your typical sweet granny and even made it into the local paper with her sunflowers! What kudos to have a picture of her standing on a step ladder next to a row of sunflowers with a watering can. The headlines read," Tallest sunflower in Reading for the second year running." Yet, she was dabbling in seances, black magic, and calling up the dead. Her string of clients, a motley crew of people desperate to contact their deceased loved ones. As a role model for me, I aspired to be like her and I remember hoping that of all the children, I would be the one who had inherited her spiritual giftings. We were always comparing who was the most like Mummy, aunty so-and-so or Nana (only wanting their good traits of course).

Growing up

Over time, the others would come home on the holidays more interested in boys, magazines, and whatever secrets they were keeping that annoying little sisters weren't privy to, no longer wanting to play. One by one they dropped out until it was just Ashley and I left. The age gap between us grew as I headed off to grammar school in my new stiff uniform, felt hat, tie, blazer, hideous brown tunic and leather satchel that dug into my shoulders, leaving Ashley behind to play with my toys and smash my recorder on the hard tile floor in the hallway in anger one day as she couldn't get it to play the notes she wanted. I only found this out years later when we were reminiscing and laughing over past antics. Then, sweetly telling Dad that it had rolled off the table onto the floor. Another time she scratched with a sharp implement "Ness was 'ere" on the coffee table, so getting me into trouble." I said nothing; I deserved the pay back after all.

Grammar school brought new responsibilities and I started to let myself in after school to an empty house. A daily routine kicked in of cooking, homework, TV, and then bed. Except on the weekends, where I applied for and got various jobs. Desperate to earn and gain independence, yearning to travel, get away, be self-sufficient, find satisfaction, joy, and FUN! My final school years came around quickly and uneventfully as I began studying for my A-levels (the final two years of study in UK schools, which weren't compulsory in those days but were a requirement for attending university).

Ashley and I were the only ones still at home. Dad was strict but fair and gave me lots of freedom. I used to sign my own notes for school and with his consent learned how to forge his signature. It was good to be granted that independence but emphasised my lack of parental boundaries and guidelines, although he was still very protective. A boyfriend once dropped me home half an hour later than my 10 pm deadline and Dad was hovering at the door as usual. The unsuspecting boyfriend tried to come in with me as he needed to use the bathroom but as he put his foot on the threshold, Dad jammed it in the door to deny him entry. "*I'm just coming in for a pee*", he lamented, at which Dad retorted, "*You're not coming in for a cup of tea at this time of night!*" Dear Dad, playing the role of mother and father, always had our interests at heart but had no wife to engage in those conversations married couples have about how best to raise the children and deal with situations that arise. The poor man had six unique hormonal personalities to handle.

In that first year of A-Levels, I made a new school friend. She introduced me to her friendship group and I would stay over and go to house parties every weekend, not having many of my own friends. I went out with a couple of boys, which was my first introduction to dating and relationships. It wasn't long, however, before one told me he didn't want to go out with me anymore because I had no friends and a boring life. Indeed, I was living my life through my friend, staying at her house and going to her parties. So, I believed the lie that I was boring and not able to form relationships. Later, my friend stopped inviting me over, which compounded the negative thoughts I had about myself, that people didn't really want to get to know me and that if they did get to know the real me, they wouldn't like what they discovered. I would even lie sometimes to people about my life to impress them.

Leaving home to go to university was going to be the answer, or so I thought. I longed to break away from the monotony of my daily life. Only about 4% of the nation went on to higher education at university in those days and it was expected that I would go, even though none of my siblings had. I had no idea what to do with my life. I had desperately tried to fit in at school, but felt self-conscious being the youngest, the smallest, the one without a mother, who knitted her own hockey sock for indoor games so as not to mark the floor, so badly in fact that it was embarrassingly full of holes. The one who tried to impress her friends by making up stories about what she had done that weekend or what presents she had received for Christmas. My aim was to leave this all behind and go to university where I'd hoped I would find people I would fit in with and the freedom to do what I wanted. What did I want?

Of course, you can't run away from your hurts and disappointments. You have to deal with them or they will pursue you. As for many young people, university proved to be a disappointment. Despite joining every club I could during Freshers Week, including *Hunt Saboteurs,* even though I had no interest or understanding about the politics of fox hunting and just wanted a fun day out running around in the woods putting the dogs off the scent! Overall, the enjoyment and friendships were forced as I tried to bond with people I had little in common with.

I had a couple of boyfriends who were probably as dysfunctional as me. When those relationships broke up, incessant tears would flow, triggering deep pain of loss and rejection that I'd never dealt with. Sometime back, I had decided to take control of my life so that I wasn't going to be hurt again. I was determined to cope using my own strength and my heart began to harden. I rarely cried, so when something touched on that deep pain inside me, the tears would flow way beyond what that situation warranted, leaving me emotionally depleted and confused.

University life brought much escapism: parties, drinking, travelling with my studies, and beginning to get self-sufficient with summer jobs. I reached the end of my time, however, not knowing what to do next. I applied for two jobs: one to be a coffee and cocoa trader and the other, a financial futures broker. Naively, I had no idea what either job entailed. Excited in my misconception I thought the first job involved travelling all over the world visiting coffee plantations. It transpired that it was a position for a trader on a commodities Exchange, while the second job was to work in financial futures in the city of London. What to do? I rang my father who advised me to take the financial job.

It was a cutthroat, fast-paced life handling money as brokers. Making a mistake could cost you your job, which it did mine as a new and inexperienced employee. Yet another incident that shook my world and plummeted my self-esteem. Finding another job was relatively easy at that time, as I worked on an Exchange trading floor, where many companies were represented. It continued to be a bumpy ride as I worked my way up the ladder. A couple of years passed and I was offered a managerial position until I shot myself in the foot. Gordon, who I had met at my first company, and I went to a work party. We got drunk and danced in an area in front of the stage which was cordoned off because there was a famous singer on the stage. Telling us not to dance there was to Gordon like putting a red rag to a bull and so, ignoring the security rules, we took to the dance floor in front of the said lady and were promptly escorted out of the building by the security guards. The following Monday I was summoned to my head office and was told I would not be getting promoted after all. Another devastating blow which compounded my self-belief as worthless, rebellious and a failure. Not only that, but everyone could see me as such. I was devastated and ashamed. When I eventually achieved a promotion, I was so afraid that I was going to be found out as incapable and a sham. I think they call it imposter syndrome. For years it caused me anguish, that I wasn't worthy to do a job and that I would be 'found out', and this was to plague me later in life in ministry roles that I was given.

More than thirty years later, the wall of fear that I would be found out and exposed was so high that it seemed impassable; until it literally came tumbling down during an encounter with Jesus. That's a later story.

Marriage and Babies

Gordon and I got married in September of 1989 and continued to live the high life, both of us earning "too much, too young." Yuppies, as the phrase was coined by the tabloids: young and upwardly mobile professional people. Thinking the world was our oyster, we made the clinical decision that it was time to have children. I didn't necessarily want children but thought it was the done thing, until I got pregnant at thirty and the baby didn't develop in the womb so that I had to go through the undignified procedure of a D&C, where they scrape anything abnormal out of the uterus. I was left empty physically and emotionally, and didn't know how to grieve, if indeed there was cause for grief. Not least because there was nothing to show for it, but also I had never properly grieved death before. With this death came the realisation that, yes, I did want children. I wanted to bring new life into the world. We decided to leave London and move to the countryside to raise a family. I was able to give up work to be a stay-at-home mum. I wanted to give my children what I hadn't had the privilege of experiencing, but it was also a great relief to lay down a career my heart had never been fully engaged in.

However, I found it hard not having a profession when surrounded by highly educated, motivated, career minded people. We would go out socially and the first question always was “what do you do?” People seemed to be impressed with status, wealth and achievement. Now I had nothing to say. I engaged in stay-at-home family life: school committees, fundraising, the social circuit, doing up the house and garden, searching for fulfilment and trying to prove that I was somebody by what I did and achieved.

Following a few years of indecision, we finally decided to give up this lifestyle of performance and the need to earn in order to maintain a certain quality of life and moved our family to the far Southwest of the country. Cornwall, once prosperous for its tin mining, now only popular with holidaymakers, artists and walkers, became our new home. Leaving the rat race, commuting, school fees and dinner parties behind, we took on big skies, sandy beaches, windswept moors and cliffs, and a new challenge:

What on earth was Gordon going to do to earn a living?

A complete change was called for as there was no investment banking down here. So after three months, we had a conversation which went something like this:

Me: *What do you like?*
Gordon: *Food and wine.*
Me: *How about working in a restaurant?*
Gordon: *It has to be a good one. The best I know is Rick Stein's.*

So began a new career in hospitality, which ranged from waiting tables to being a sommelier, to being an avid student of viticulture to teacher in the industry, not necessarily in that order.

Gordon had given up his big career and I had given up everything that defined me. Not feeling like I ever had anything interesting to contribute or that others enjoyed my company, I felt I was becoming invisible and believed the lie that nobody wanted to listen to me speak or to the music I liked. I also thought I had to put my desires on hold because as a mother, obviously the children came first in that season. I was becoming less and less; I was shrinking.

What was wrong with me? Why didn't people want to hang out with me, or so I thought. Why didn't I want to hang out with them? I even sometimes felt others didn't see me. I have walked right past someone I know who is walking towards me and have blanked them as I assumed they can't see me! It reminds me of playing hide and seek with Ashley when she was about three or four. I counted to fifty, then went to look for her but she had stayed right in my view with her hands over her face.

"What on earth are you doing?, I bemoaned,
You were supposed to run off and hide".
"But I am hidden," she sweetly replied. I can't see you,
therefore you can't see me".

That is what I did. I used to try not to see people, thinking they could not see me; believing the lie that I was invisible. If you go into a room full of people and you think they're not going to like you or want to talk to you, you put up a wall and somehow, they sense it and they don't open up to you or even notice you, which just compounds the lie you already believe about yourself, that people don't want to get to know you.

This affected my ability to develop friendships, and I was really unhappy and searching for acceptance and value.

I found my identity in the church. I took on whatever role I was asked to do, be it Sunday school teacher, prayer group leader, fund raiser or coffee maker. You might think that was a good thing, but again I was finding validation in performance. I was one person while at church with the Holy Spirit flowing and feeling God's presence and another person at home as a mum and wife who would get short with the kids and row with her husband, who would get upset and depressed over seemingly very little. I couldn't reconcile the two lives that I had and knew my spiritual life needed to be merged with my actual home life. I asked God to help me as I felt I was living two very different lives.

He answered me by allowing me to go through some very difficult experiences in a church I attended until the church fell apart and I had nowhere to go. Gradually, I realised that all the church programs I was involved with were no longer satisfying and I withdrew from the groups and ministries I had joined in Cornwall. World lockdown came with the pandemic in 2020, by which time I had already been in my own personal lockdown for a couple of years.

I can see now that during the twenty years thus far as a Christian, I was always trying to perform, and I still carried deep wounds of rejection and abandonment. Over a long period of time, God stripped me of all of it. He needed to get me back to the foundations so I could discover who He had made me to be and rebuild from there.

In 2018, He told me to batten down the hatches and spend time with Him, beginning a journey of healing, restoration and learning that my identity was in Him. I had to have courage to go against the flow of what everyone else was doing at the time. I knew He was calling me; somehow I knew deep down that this was so key to seeing a huge transformation and shift in my life. It was time.

Trying to Fit

It's the present day and I'm walking my dog as I have done for the last twenty years on the cliffs near my home in Cornwall. Bingo, our second dog, the first was a chocolate lab named Dizzy who was as silly as her name suggests, runs ahead and sticks her nose in the gorse. A clever black lab who thinks she is either male or human most of the time. Unexpectedly bounding into our lives with the pit for Dizzy barely dug, the soil on top still loose and bare. Gordon worked into the evening breaking through the hard ground on the garden path where he decided she would find her final resting place, sweating and toiling to get it done before nightfall, his way of grieving.

I can't believe we have lived here so long. Prior to that, my childhood was seemingly one of constantly moving until it stretched to eight years and finally to twenty. I've just begun to write my book and as I walk in the wild open spaces of this ancient land, memories open up, coming in thick and fast.

Already, I'm sifting through them, discarding any that might offend, rock the boat, or face truths. I'm vetting them, ensuring they are all "fine", doing exactly what my father used to do.

As I recall the eiderdown story and his calm reaction, I think of the day when he sat on the sofa in my new marital home and I tried to discuss with him some of the problems in our relationship that had affected me growing up. I said sorry for my part as I carefully shared memories, without going into too many details, skirting around them to begin with but making clear enough the things he could have done differently, giving him little room for manoeuvre. My words hung in the air, like a damp sheet brushing past his head, trying to stick as he ducked under the washing line, the only way through the backyard to the exit, to be irritatingly pushed aside before it plastered his face. His face flickered with the tiniest expression as though he was remembering, processing something long forgotten. Then incredulously it was gone, face blank, he asking me what I was talking about. He never could face deep conversations. A mouldy abandoned sandwich squashed back into the folds of the eiderdown. That's where he was going to leave it. I was left hung and dry.

That's an aside, wandering from the path where all is going fine until you find yourself adrift, caught in brambles that snag on your clothing as you retrace your steps and try to pull away.

As I ponder about all the homes I have lived in, the places I have had the privilege of visiting, I wonder if that gave me my love of travel to exotic faraway places and the sense of adventure of trying out new things. Even as a student I would spend all my earnings from holiday jobs backpacking around the Greek islands or visiting the Far East and this continued when I met Gordon, who also has a love for travel.

The excitement of going on an aeroplane to new and faraway places, the adventures to be had, the people to meet, all excited and enticed me. Sometimes, I look back and think I was searching for something that I couldn't find in the dreariness and monotony of my home life and I couldn't wait to leave and go to university, to begin a new adventure, hoping that I would find what I was looking for–whatever that was. What I didn't know back then was that it isn't what is happening in our environment that can give us true fulfilment, but what is happening inside of us and how we perceive the world. I also know now that a sense of adventure and exploration is part of who I am and can embrace that. Even at a young age, like most young people, I was looking for that next fun thing to do.

The penchant for travel and adventure followed me everywhere and I am grateful to my father for the freedom he gave me to try out new things on my own; the encouragement to step out and be independent. However, combining that with not having the discipline and guidelines a mother provides, not really knowing my boundaries, and also the constant search within me for fulfilment, led me to make stupid decisions. Once on a school trip to Germany our coach stopped at a café. I was about fourteen and there was a group of young French people, maybe seventeen or eighteen years old, on the next table of our roadside cafe who invited us to have a ride on one of their party's motorbikes. Now of course all the other girls declined the offer, but this to me was most enticing. So, my teacher came out of the café to see me roaring off up the road on the back of a stranger's motorbike. Thankfully, I was returned unscathed but had to spend the rest of the trip sitting on the front seat of the coach next to the driver and I couldn't really see what I had done wrong. Later, when my Russian studies took me to the Soviet Union, it was such an adventure. I loved trading on the black market, meeting people in the park to swap clothes and trade currency, being lowered out of second floor windows on sheets tied together after curfew, and going outside the city which was our permitted boundary. Another time, I was stopped by a plain clothed policeman in the city we were touring, questioned about having a party on the beach with some Russian students after curfew. Thankfully, he had got the wrong night so I could genuinely deny the accusation!

I loved the sense of adventure and giddiness from pushing the boundaries.

If I got stuck in the monotony of a place, I wanted to move on, but there were seasons when moving on wasn't an option. In such times, I sometimes felt confined and stuck.

Either way, whether moving or staying, I never really felt as though I fit. The uprooting every few years, especially in childhood, coupled with the loss of key figures in my life, gave me a sense of not belonging, not finding my own people, so to speak, despite always looking to fit as I went from one place to the next like a nomad.

Chapter 4
WOULD I EVER FIT?

He has made everything beautiful in its time.
Also He has put eternity in their hearts (Ecclesiastes 3:11 NKJV)

There are some things about where we fit that cannot be changed, such as our place of birth, the family we're born into, what number we are among our siblings, our nationality, sex physical attributes, personality, the society, religion and culture, our year of birth and so on. To start, we are moulded and influenced by all the above. We try to fit in, accepting that all around us is the norm. I was desperately trying to find my place and hold on to my mother and embrace everything about her.

Dad was the youngest of five, an Englishman, a soldier, a war child, lost his father young. Mummy was the youngest of eleven Portuguese children living in Macau and Hong Kong. Dad was raised a nominal Christian in the Church of England, mummy as a practising Catholic. They were naive and young when they married and quickly began their large family. All these and being born into a large lively family, number five of six, would have influenced me and how I fit.

As a baby, I got labels, being told I was scrawny and that I cried a lot. Later, I was labelled spoiled, called 'weed' because I was small and skinny and my surname was Weedon. I was the youngest during my time at boarding school and I got very spoiled, or so I'm told. At school I was called clever, a chatterbox, and sweet which is fine as a child but not years later at work! I exasperated Dad as I was always asking questions, was argumentative and stubborn. These are some of the labels I was given that influenced what I thought of myself and how I fitted.

I remember feeling so different from the other children at my school for having been born and raised in my formative years in Africa. I was strange, almost exotic to them. "Did you *live in a mud* hut?" some asked in wide eyed innocence. On the one hand, it made me feel good that they were interested in me as I wanted to be accepted and included. On the other hand, I didn't like to feel as though I was the same as them and there was always the nagging fear of rejection because I was different–an outsider. The headmistress announced on my first day at school that Mummy had died. She was trying to be kind so that everyone would be sensitive and understanding, but I didn't want that kind of notoriety and attention!

Another label was over my nationality and whether I was English or Nigerian. Friends would argue about which one I was depending on the criteria they believed determines nationality. I would always proudly say that I was half-Portuguese. When we lived in Africa, I was an English girl but when we lived in England, I was an African; I was torn between two cultures, two ways of life.

One of my personal experiences that compounded the feeling of not fitting in was of having my ears pierced at the tender age of four. Vanessa should have her ears pierced, my mother was told by the cook's wife, who announced that her own daughters had pierced ears. It was very simple, and she would do it. I couldn't have been more than four years old, but was listening, eyes boggling and ears flapping to the narrative unfolding above and around me. My older sisters were away at a Catholic boarding school in England where they were, in theory, getting a decent education; so, they would not be exposed to what you might consider barbarism–not yet anyway. A few years later, when pierced ears became all the rage, one of them fainted having hers done in front of the bathroom mirror and hit her head on the sink as she went down. Thankfully, she lived to tell the tale with minimal damage save a bruised cheek and ego. I wasn't able to escape so easily. So, handing the cook's wife a needle and thread my mother permitted the piercing of my tender little lobes, which then spent several weeks with string in the holes until they had healed and I was given my first pair of tiny gold hoops to wear.

I thought all of this was normal until attending my first school in England when I was eight; just to discover that I was the only child in the school with pierced ears. That was one of many times in my life when I felt different, strange, and complicated. It fuelled that inner voice telling me I wasn't how I should be and wasn't therefore accepted or acceptable. Of course, by the time I was in my second year at senior school, every girl in my class had persuaded their parents to let them have pierced ears and I was no longer the weird one who they didn't know how to place in their world. Some had thought I might be a gypsy because of the hoops. People said I was African, some with undertones of prejudice (although actually I was, according to my place of birth) and in their ignorance asked me if I'd lived in a mud hut. Then, to have no mother or proper upbringing as some would consider proper, one of my friends told me her mum thought I was a "wild child" with no discipline and they didn't want their daughter to hang out with me. Children can deliver cruel blows in their naivety and candour.

When you don't fit in, you feel insecure, unliked, and unlovable, which can lead to loneliness, anger, hopelessness and despair. Some people retreat in on themselves and others, like me, decide to take fierce independent action. Either way you begin to die inside. You stop being a voice and having an opinion. You attract domineering and controlling people, all the while you are desperately trying to blend in.

In my case, I was always on the move, so never able to really put down roots or to get to know people for long to build lasting relationships. I never knew which group of people I fit in with, so I learned to adapt and blend in. I picked up accents and tried to copy the behaviours of my peers–like a chameleon. It was exhausting! That's probably why I learned to speak with a

Nigerian accent and could identify Nigerians abroad. It's also why when asked by a friend what I got for Christmas, I started to fabricate a ridiculous story about getting a toy horse with accessories when in fact I'd been given a doll. She knew that I was lying and kept probing me with questions which made it worse. I could feel her eyes burning into me and felt so embarrassed and ashamed for lying. Trying to fit in, yet feeling like you never belong is tiring. Finally, it seems easier to become reclusive, to move on and forget the people you met before. A life of self-preservation, rootlessness and restlessness became the norm.

What if, wherever we went, we carried something so valuable inside of us that it doesn't matter where we live or what knocks we experience? What if home is where the heart is, as the saying goes, or that we carry eternity in our hearts? What if we can find home wherever we are? What if we could fit wherever we went because we are secure in our identity?

Jesus of Nazareth was one man who definitely had nowhere to belong and yet He was the most secure man in history who fulfilled His purpose and had the greatest impact on mankind of any person to have ever lived. Yes, to many He is God who can do all things, but he did this as a man. Jesus, fully God, left his heavenly home and took on flesh. Born in Bethlehem to Mary and Joseph, He was raised in Nazareth, was later rejected by his own people as he began to fulfil His destiny. "What good can come out of Nazareth?" they asked, only willing to see Him as the son of a carpenter. They couldn't see his potential or greatness and rejected him as the promised saviour of the world. He then spent approximately three years in a small geographical area proclaiming the good news, healing the sick, raising the dead and casting out demons. Always on the move, he said the son of man had nowhere to lay his head. After only three years of ministry, He was crucified, buried and ascended to heaven where He is now seated at the Father's right hand. He gave us the Holy Spirit to make a home in us, so that Jesus could be with us always.

During His short ministry on earth Jesus was mistreated, maligned, misunderstood, and rejected. He spent His years of ministry moving from one town to another. Yet He was completely secure in the knowledge of who He was and what he was sent to do on the earth. Being fully man and fully God you may think His divinity helped Him, but actually He had to overcome the same struggles that you and I face because He chose to lay down His divine rights and live as a man. In His humanity He had all the same emotions, feelings, needs and struggles; yet He overcame. He demonstrated that we can too.

There are other notable characters in the Bible: David, Joseph, and Moses who, despite their experience of rejection, homelessness, being misunderstood and wrongly labelled, learned to be secure in who they were and what they were called to do.

David spent many hours out in the fields, the youngest of several brothers, tending the sheep. He sang and played the lyre and I imagine he spent many hours worshipping and talking with God. His older brothers treated him with contempt, but he knew who he was as he spent many years alone with the sheep developing his skills and honing his character. He knew God and the call on his life. Through protecting the sheep, he learned how to battle lions and bears. When he took on Goliath he didn't put on the King's armour or show fear. He was confident that he could slay the giant because he knew his God and was secure enough not to take on someone else's ways, but to use his slingshot which he was experienced in. Even though the prophet Samuel told him he would be King, he didn't rule for another thirty years, and ended up on the run as a fugitive. Despite this, he didn't give up on his destiny and was also recognised by others as king who chose to follow him even before he was crowned.

Joseph had many older brothers who treated him harshly. He had dreams and desires which he tried to share with his older brothers but came across arrogantly; so they cast him out of their father's home and packed him off with slavers who took him to Egypt. There he spent many years as a servant and then in Pharaoh's dungeons, never losing his faith and trusting in God until his time of release, deliverance, and promotion.

What of Moses? He was born to a Hebrew slave in Egypt when Pharaoh ordered the killing of all Hebrew babies. Pharaoh was afraid that the Hebrew race was growing too large. Moses' mother hid him in bulrushes along the Nile River where he was discovered and taken into Pharaoh's household to be raised as a Prince of Egypt. One day he discovered his roots and killed a man who had killed a Hebrew. This was the start of him stepping into his identity.

Can you see the pattern here? Jesus, David, Joseph, Moses; none of them fit. They were like a swan amongst ducklings. As they began to discover the calling on their lives, they acted impetuously. They got themselves in trouble; Moses killed an Egyptian who was arguing with a Hebrew. He was trying to defend his people and ended up fleeing. Joseph told his brothers they would bow down to him, so they sold him into slavery. David had to go on the run and hide in caves because he was being pursued by the King who was fearful that David was going to take over his position. Only Jesus moved in the perfect timing of God. The other commonality they had was their personal relationship with God. In all my search for finding my place, my tribe, and my peace, I never found it until I met Jesus and discovered that I had been looking in all the wrong places and doing all the wrong things.

Chapter 5
MEETING JESUS ON THE JOURNEY: THE WAY TO HEALING AND WHOLENESS

I am the way and the truth and the Life (John 14:6 NIV)

People come and go in our lives but Jesus is not someone you want to meet and then part with. There is an incident in the Bible in Luke 24:13-35 after Jesus had been crucified and buried. Everyone was talking about this famous preacher/prophet and along a road not far from Jerusalem two men were walking, animatedly discussing the events of the previous few days. As they walked and talked Jesus came alongside them and joined in with their conversation, yet they didn't recognise who He was. It was only later, after He had explained the scriptures with them, talked about Himself, shared a meal, broke bread and left did they realise who had been with them. It's the same for us. Jesus could pass right by. You could even read this book and meet Jesus in the pages but then let Him go at the end without wanting to have Him permanently by your side. He is a gentleman and never barges His way in but waits to be invited, but once you invite Him into your life, He is there to stay.

He will never leave you again. It's not a passing moment as He comes to make His abode forever.

Until my personal encounter with Jesus, I was what you would call a nominal Christian. Many westerners say they are Christians but don't actually know God. I certainly didn't know that Jesus was alive, and I could have a relationship with Him. Once I began a relationship with Jesus, I discovered that I fit into a new family. I learned that I am a daughter of God and can call him Abba-Father. I am a co-heir with Christ. I am no longer a slave. I am the Bride of Christ and I get all the benefits of being a daughter of the King of Kings with the accompanying blessings and promises. I am now righteous because I take on Christ's identity. God has many names, which express His attributes: the Lord is my righteousness, provider, healer, deliverer, and so many more. This is now part of my family, identity and where I fit. Jesus, the Firstborn, has a genealogy going all the way back to Adam and Eve, which we can now partake of by faith.

As I began to discover how I fit into the family of God, I also began to see who Vanessa was within that family as He began to walk with me and reveal Himself. He is the Shepherd and He says "my sheep know my voice" (John 10:27). Before knowing Him, I was scattered adrift, not knowing what I was going to do with my life. I had too many things going on: hard work, fast paced city life, drinking, partying, and smoking. Even though I was only thirty, I was tired of my lifestyle. So when my sister Stephanie told me about her living relationship with Jesus I discovered there was a longing in my heart to have what she had and to lay down all my striving. Until then no one had told me Jesus was alive. In all my years of going to church on Sundays as a child, I didn't know He was alive, kicking and knocking on the door of my heart.

As I look back on the journey of my life, despite not knowing him until adulthood, He knew me and He was always with me watching over me. With this new understanding that He is always with us, I was able to look at my life from His perspective and re-write the narrative of my past because when He is with you, everything changes.

As I walked with Jesus and began to know His character and how He perceived me, the most impactful thing I discovered and experienced was His love. I realised that God is love, therefore all He does is founded in love; that He loves me unconditionally and without measure. The revelation unfolded that my identity comes from how He sees me as His beloved. No other names and labels are as profound and impactful. No other person can tell me who I am. There is no better place to be than in Him. This is the foundation for our identity. Knowing our identity as God sees us is crucial to finding our value, capabilities, and purpose. This will be discussed at greater length in the following chapters in light of my experience.

PART TWO:

OBSERVATIONS AND LESSONS LEARNED

Chapter 6
THE IMPORTANCE OF IDENTITY

"I am who You say I am"
Hillsong Worship

Identity refers to our sense of who we are as individuals and as members of social groups. It also refers to our sense of how others may perceive and label us. We develop ideas about our identities and that of others through our interactions with people close to us, like our family, friends, schools, other institutions, the media, and our encounters with other individuals. Sometimes we don't even realise that we have these ideas because we don't remember learning them.

Personal identity refers to the unique ways that we define ourselves. It can be answered by the question, "Who am I?" Answering this question is an important part of growing up. One person might choose to emphasise their family, religion, and interests when describing their identity. Another might emphasise their race, neighbourhood, and job as important parts of who they are. Our personal identity consists of all the things that we believe make us, us.

Identity also depends upon how other individuals and society label us. So the answer to who I am depends in large part on who the world says I am. Who do my parents say I am? Who do my peers say I am? What message is reflected back to me in the faces and voices of my teachers, neighbours, and co-workers? What do I learn from the media about myself? How am I represented in the cultural images around me, or am I missing from the picture altogether?

As children we often put on plays to amuse ourselves and entertain Dad and this involved dressing up, putting on accents and taking on behaviours, perhaps a limp and an *aha me hearties*, or a sparkling princess dress with tiara. My poor brother was even once dressed up by Stephanie as a girl and, suffice to say that from then on he told us categorically that he was going to be a burglar when he grew up.

We are born into some of the characteristics that give us our identity: name, nationality, family, religion, tribe, and colour of our skin. This identity is shared with our immediate family. We also have a set of characteristics which allows us to be definitively and uniquely recognisable such as, our physical traits, fingerprints, hair type, weaknesses (disabilities), strengths, our first name and our personality type. These tend to be unchangeable.

Some parts of our identity may remain the same throughout our life, such as the form and colour of our eyes, fingerprints, and our sex. Other parts of our identity are more fluid and change as we move from childhood through adolescence and into adulthood as we interact with and are influenced by different social groups.

Yet it is often our families and those we have known for the longest who find it hard to see us in any other way than what they know. To our children we will always be Mum and how they see us is according to the role we had in their lives. Once, when my kids were little, we discussed what the word *vocation* means and I explained that it is what you do as your main occupation. My youngest, who was about five at the time, asked me, "Mummy, is your vocation to wash the dishes then?" Understandably, I did have my 'marigolds' on and was at the sink at the time!

In ancient civilisations and in many eastern cultures, identity is based foremost on family, tribe, origins, and bloodline. In the Bible, genealogy is very important. You only need to look at the long list of *begats* to see this. When someone was introduced, it was usually as so and so, son or daughter of... Then the names of parents, grandparents, great grandparents were listed. This was very important to know as when people made treaties and covenants, it was vital to understand who they were making them with and by looking at their ancestors they could see if this was good soil to sow into or not, and what their relationships were like historically, for example, whether there were any feuds.

Jesus's genealogy was clearly established by looking at both Mary and Joseph's family lines, so there can be no disputing His ancestry, which went back to King David from whose line the Messiah was promised.

Our identity in modern western civilisation has become more to do with what we do rather than the family we are born into. Take a social gathering. When you are introduced to someone you may be told, this is Jane, a nurse from Manchester. On a chat show, the contestant may be announced as Bob from Derby, a business consultant married to Jen with three children.

I certainly anchored my identity on what I did, wearing my job description like a label across my forehead which made me feel valued and significant.

Later, God began to strip these labels away, one by one, until I was left floundering like a ship at sea.

O you afflicted one, Tossed with tempest, and not comforted,
Behold, I will lay your stones with colourful gems,
And lay your foundations with sapphires. (Isaiah 54:11, NKJV)

There are people throughout history who have rebelled against the parts of their identity they've inherited. This is often as a new generation breaks away from the acceptable norm and culture of the time. Women in strict religious societies, and teenagers against their parents' generation are typical examples.

We can have what can be termed as an identity crisis, where we become confused about our identity and this can make us unstable and insecure.

According to the book of Exodus, Moses was born in Egypt to Hebrew parents, who set him afloat on the Nile in a reed basket to save him from an edict calling for the death of all newborn Hebrew males. Found by the pharaoh's daughter, he was reared in the Egyptian court. As he began to discover his Hebrew roots and realised his own people were being treated appallingly by the Egyptians who had raised him, he decided to take action but ended up killing a brutal Egyptian taskmaster; whereupon he fled to Midian, where God revealed Himself in a burning bush and called Moses to deliver the Israelites from Egypt. It took forty years in the wilderness as a shepherd to get Egypt out of Moses and to train him up as the deliverer of his people. During that time God revealed himself to Moses and told Moses who He was and what His destiny was.

When we were growing up, we knew a family who had adopted their son at birth. Philip was dearly loved by his adoptive parents, but when you saw him with them and their biological daughter, they were like chalk and cheese. Even the way he spoke was different; betraying that he was from another class in the British class system. This young man was fortunate to be raised in a family who affirmed his unique personality traits and giftings even though they may not have understood him and he became a pilot in the Royal Air Force after a childhood obsession with aeroplanes and all things military.

The story of the ugly duckling is very familiar, who, when hatched along with his brothers and sisters, is ridiculed and ostracised because they perceive him as ugly due to his differences. He wanders alone through the fall and winter, suffers from fear, loneliness, and sadness. In the spring he flies away from the marsh and meets up with a group of swans and realises that he too has become a beautiful swan. A happy ending as he discovers who he is after finding his own kind.

If we grow up surrounded by those who always affirm us and encourage us, then we will generally have a positive view of ourselves and will develop self-worth. Conversely, we can also have a negative view of ourselves when we don't fit in and when people give us labels, which impacts how we live, relate to others, and what we achieve of our purpose in life.

Pain cycles and difficulties of not knowing our identity

You can't put a round peg in a square hole, so the saying goes and that's quite true. Have you ever watched a little child trying to put the round plastic block in the triangle or square shaped hole in their toy shape sorter? No matter how hard they try, it's never going to fit.

That's the same with us. Unfortunately, we may live much of our life before we actually realise that trying to ram one shape into another shaped hole isn't going to work. We find ourselves having made career, relationship, and other life choices that have put us on a trajectory so far from where we'd really like to be. We have tried to find fulfilment from what we do when in reality we have inner longings and regrets.

I believe that a root cause stems from making life choices not knowing our true identity or what we were actually created to do in life. We have unique gifts and callings. Yet, metaphorically speaking, we try to put the round peg in the square hole as we take on careers that we think are expected of us, but in actuality make us feel like imposters. We learn to speak in Nigerian accents and pretend we got a toy horse for Christmas instead of the doll we were actually given. Like chameleons, we adapt to people and situations to try and belong. In short, we lie to ourselves and others about who we really are and pursue careers and interests that if we were really honest with ourselves, do not fulfil us.

We end up hanging out with people we have nothing in common with who don't understand us. We sometimes try to say what we want to do but don't feel heard or we get misunderstood. I referred to Joseph earlier who was destined to save nations, yet he dared to share his dreams with his older brothers and they just thought he was being arrogant. They hated him so much that they gave him away to slave traders who took him to a far country where he was raised as a citizen of that nation, obscuring his true identity. After many years of pain, suffering and refining he eventually fulfilled the call on his life and his identity was restored and he was accepted and reunited with his brothers.

If we feel shut down enough times, we stop trying to speak, we lose our voice as we believe we have nothing to say of value that others will be interested in. We can become invisible, door mats, and attract dominating people into our lives who intentionally or unwittingly coerce and control.

In our relationships, we are attracted to other lost souls, looking for affirmation of who we are from those who are as broken and displaced as us.

We can become fiercely independent and determined to do our own thing, becoming a closed book as hearts become hardened and calloused.

As we believe lies about ourselves that we are: unlikeable, people don't want to hang out with us, there is something wrong with us, or people don't even see us, then we actually can become invisible. You've heard the saying that the loneliest place to be is in a crowded room. If we go into a room full of people with expectations that they won't like us or want to talk to us, this puts up a wall and an invisible sign that says "stay away" which people sense and so avoid us. This can compound the negative lies we already believe about ourselves.

We end up always on the move, maybe not geographically as in my case, but moving on from one relationship to the next, having shallow friendships and not letting people get to know us as if they knew the real us they wouldn't like us.

It becomes hard to form deep friendships, not least because we think people will find out what we're really like and will reject us.

We have unfulfilled yearnings and desires which we try to live through our children, compelling them to take on hobbies or to study subjects that we always wanted to do but never did.

The lies we believe often distort what actually happened in our past. All the above have been my experience. The good news is that I discovered how to rewrite the narrative, which I will share later.

Chapter 7
THE RELATIONSHIP BETWEEN A MOTHER AND CHILD

"But we were gentle among you,
just as a nursing mother cherishes her own children."
1 Thess. 2:7 (NKJV)

The first people who should speak into our life and help us find our unique personality and identity are our parents.

It is through our families that we are nurtured and grow in a safe environment. Families are central to God's plan for His children. They are the fundamental building blocks of strong societies. Families are where we can feel love and learn how to love others. Life is tough, and we need people we can lean on. Home should be a safe haven where we receive love, advice, and support. This should be the experience of every child from the moment of conception.

Scientific research is increasingly proving what mothers of newborn babies have been instinctively doing since time began. After cutting the umbilical cord, moving the child to the mother's chest is an incredibly beneficial way to welcome a baby for both mother and child. The skin-to-skin contact causes a release in oxytocin–known as the love hormone. This and other hormones released help mum and baby bond emotionally. It sparks intense feelings of love and protectiveness in the mother which are crucial for the well-being of both mother and baby. Where babies have been starved of love and affection, this being particularly true in some cultures if the babies are born with disabilities or placed in orphanages, there have subsequently been marked improvements in the children's wellbeing and demeanour when caregivers have realised the importance of infant bonding. Programmes teaching mothers to spend more time holding their babies have had a significant positive impact on the wellbeing of mothers and children; especially as the babies become less distressed which in turn calms the mother and helps her to bond with her newborn. African mothers understand the importance of carrying their babies on their backs to soothe, comfort and bring security.

According to Healthway Medical, being a mother is one of the most important roles a woman can ever play. In the first few years of a child's life, the few people they have close contact with will have the greatest impact on their development in early childhood. Studies have shown that early childhood is a period in which developmentally, a child is learning a lot from their surroundings and the people around them. This is the child's window of learning which will impact their growing years and they will thrive when they have a secure and positive relationship with people and especially their parents. Mothers play a crucial role in caring for, loving, teaching and training them. Being loved from this early stage will help a child feel secure in their identity later.

Of course, not all mothers are able to give the love and nurture a child needs due to a variety of reasons: circumstances, immaturity, mother-wounds and so on. Simply put, there are also intentionally bad mothers, although the cause of this may be rooted in their own lack of mothering.

In her book *The Deborah Anointing* (referring to Deborah who led the tribes of Israel in the Old Testament), Michelle McClain-Walters believes that mothering is needed today because mothers have been losing the ability and desire to nurture life. There are many news reports of women's cruelty, even murder, to their own children. Eve, who God called the mother of all living things, had the role of nourishing, nurturing, and giving life. She is our example.

According to Michelle McClain-Walters, "There must be a recapturing of the essence of motherhood." She says we must be intentional about training our daughters to be godly mothers in the Kingdom. To nurture involves "the act of nursing." It means to suckle or nourish. It also means "to further the development of." God designed human nature to be nurtured by a mother and a father. The dismantling of the family unit was the beginning of the decline of morality in many western nations. Nurturing is essential for the health of humanity.

Michelle McClain-Walters emphasises the importance of Deborah as a mother, who did not see greatness in emulating the qualities of manhood. Instead, with kindness and faith, she sought to be a mother in Israel: a giver of life and a nurturer of her people.

> ***"The mothering anointing is returning to this land. This facet of the Deborah anointing is the ability to nurture a generation. One of the major causes of rebellion in the youth of our society is rejection and lack of guidance." She continues, "Modern day Deborahs will be like teachers who nurture the next generation's creativity. They will understand that in order to produce good fruit in our children, they must carefully nurture the vine." (Michelle McClain-Walters)***

Impact of Losing a Mother

I was blessed to have my mother until I was five years old, but after that was influenced to varying degrees by mother types who passed through my life. This included my older sisters with their maternal, protective instinct over us "little ones," as we were known. Despite the fact that my father never remarried, nor dare he bring a girlfriend home because of the scrutiny from his five daughters. Nicole developed her maternal instincts by practising on all our dolls rather than her younger siblings, probably reeling from the experience when Romayne once cut Nicole's fringe and as she kept trying to straighten it, Nicole ended up with no fringe at all. So, lovingly and painstakingly Nicole cut each doll's hair off and painted their nails with permanent felt tip pens. She went on to be a wonderful caring nurse and mother, so I forgive her for practising on my dolls!

Even before Mummy's death, because we were a large family, I expect she and Dad relied on Stephanie and Romayne to help with us younger ones. Of course, when she died, that role was thrust upon them even more, forcing them into responsibilities that they should not have had to bear, still being children themselves.

Older siblings acting as parents can have a positive impact as they help to meet missing needs but can be skewed in application. My siblings competed over who was in charge of whom and, not having experienced it themselves, did not understand that love should be consistent, unconditional and shared equally. It was no one's fault, just children trying to work out love and life. I, in turn, tried to mother my little sister, or rather lord it over her, as in the sweeties episode and the time when I hastily shoved her across the road to save her from oncoming traffic. My intentions were good, but a parent who witnessed the incident reported me to the headmistress and my humiliating punishment was to stand in the corner of the school hall with my back to everyone during assembly. How ashamed and misunderstood I felt.

Later, when I became a mother myself, I realised I didn't have the usual blueprint for raising a family and it is a wonder that my siblings and I have managed to parent eighteen children who have all turned into wonderful adults. I admit that I made mistakes but one thing that I can categorically say is that I have fiercely loved my children.

When we lost Mummy, mothers in our neighbourhood rallied round to help the handsome bachelor with six children in tow, bereft from losing his young wife. Many women living in Africa were part of a generation of stay-at-home mums who willingly wanted to offer their time but the romantic notion of swooping in to help, despite all the best intentions, soon waned. Meals weren't needed as we had a cook and home-help and the likelihood of Dad finding a new partner, even as time went by, was seriously hampered by the fact that he had six children.

In fact, any relationship Dad later wanted to develop was doomed to fail as there were five daughters ready to dissect and pull apart any poor unsuspecting woman. Romantic notions of the heroine entering our lives like Maria in the Sound of Music to rescue the family and have us all singing on the mountain in our outfits made from old curtains were soon dashed. These women were sent packing, unable to cope with our scrutiny, leaving Dad to resort to nannies. We children unconsciously became a tight knit unit.

The Impact of Mother Figures in my Life

I have heard it said that you can't be a good father if you haven't learned how to be a son. Likewise, you can't be a good mother without being a good daughter. Fathers are meant to instill identity. Mothers are responsible for nurturing and fanning the flame to that identity. Despite lacking this from the age of five onwards, as I look back, I can see how God weaved mother figures into my life. Some mother figures berated me. The impact of one negative word or action on a child looking for love and affirmation can not be underestimated. But there were also moments where I connected with women who validated me with tenderness and love, however brief our interaction.

Take the beautiful sixteen-year-old Irish girl who babysat for us and would spend hours sitting on the floor colouring with me; or the mother who kindly offered to give me a lift to an eighth birthday party, but who never came, leaving me bereft and confused in Nana's hallway. It may seem so trivial to most people, but it just confirmed to the little girl in me that I was alone and there was no one who really cared about me.

Then there was the mother who told my friend that she didn't want her daughter to spend time with me as I was a bad influence being motherless. I was only seven!

The mother who invited me to her daughter's birthday party even though I didn't know a soul, had kind intentions. The instructions for the first game were given and all the children scattered excitedly to various parts of the garden, except for me, who was left standing, not having understood a word of the instructions which were spoken in Dutch.

Much damage is done unintentionally; a sharp word here, a thoughtless action there, and these can accumulate to influence the narrative of your life. I'm not sure if I remember the incident when the family left me crawling about on the floor as I was told about it so many times, but it reinforced the belief I had in later years that I needed to look after myself. So, increasingly keeping others at a distance I became an expert in self-sufficiency.

Then there were the surrogate mothers or nannies that passed through our lives for longer periods. Ashley, as I said earlier, was taken into the care of Mummy's sister, Wanda, until we unanimously asked Dad not to give her up.

It was then that Dad employed a new nanny, Karen, and took her out with us to Nigeria. It took Dad several weeks to work out what she was up to. Karen liked to have male friends and she would drag us around in the car to her various clandestine meetings and rendezvous. I remember one occasion jostling with Ashley as we peered through the back of the car window, while she talked to and kissed a rather large swarthy Greek man. On another occasion a young English man, Stephen, who didn't realise quite how out of his depth he was, came to the house. They shut themselves in Karen's bedroom and made us wait outside, bribing us meanwhile with strips of gooey flat toffees called goody goodies, which she passed through the crack under the door, hoping we would stop irritating her.

Another of Mummy's sisters, Terry, who was also my godmother, would visit us from the United States where she lived with her American husband. As her goddaughter, she showered me with time, attention and gifts. I lapped this up, just like our cat when firmly stroked behind his ear. Later I invited Terry to stand in for Mummy at our wedding, but that relationship ended abruptly due to a family spat over the seating plan; offence was taken and I never heard from her again, only to find out much later that she had died. Decades later I went to Aunty Wanda's funeral, the aunt who had taken Ashley in during Dad's hour of need. Not having been to my own mother's funeral, I found it strangely moving as I felt like I was saying goodbye to Mummy properly for the first time.

The other aunt I loved was Dad's sister, Pamela, who I got to know when I lived at Nana's for a year following our return from Nigeria after the nanny saga. Pamela often visited and I have memories of her dancing with me in the front room and twirling me around. I thrived on the attention. Pamela was going through a breakdown which I didn't discern as a child as she showered me with love and attention, but in her unhinged state fell out with Nana and stopped visiting! I didn't see her again until many decades later and never understood the reason for the breakup between mother and daughter.

Nana's death from falling down the stairs a couple of years later when we were no longer living with her was just another devastating blow, but by then I had learned to control and suppress the pain and grief of loss.

Over the years, God brought friends into my life who have sometimes been like a sister, and other times like a mother. They have been there for me as listeners, mentors, and comforters; but occasionally, I've attracted unhealthy relationships because they want to mother me from their own woundedness and have tried to give me more than I actually want or need from them.

The Positive Influences From NOT Having a Mother

Unless you know what it is like to grow up in a healthy home with loving parents you actually don't realise you are missing out. I had a sunny temperament, even though I was a little hot headed! I had tenacity and perseverance when used the right way, which are character traits that have stood me well. I may have missed out on early nurturing, after school clubs, a welcome when I came in from school, a kiss and a hug when I was hurt, someone to tell me about growing up into womanhood, and so on; but I reaped the benefit of three older experienced sisters, a protective brother and a loving father in our close knit family. I had an independence and zest for life fostered by the freedom I had from not having a mum at home.

Indeed, there were some great advantages, or so I felt in my teenage years as I became more independent. We had a lot of freedom as children. In Nigeria, while the older ones were at boarding school I was often left to my own devices and had the security of a large enclosed garden protected by our watchman.

I had a very good relationship with my father as a child. I think I reminded him of Mummy and while the others were away at boarding school we developed a good rapport. As I grew older, he even allowed me to forge his signature so I could sign my own letters for school. While lenient in many ways, there was a line we knew not to cross. One incident we used to reminisce about (we were always reminiscing, trying to hold onto memories that bonded us and brought us joy) was when we had collectively made Dad angry. He'd finally had enough and raised his hand to slam it on the table but had forgotten he was holding a glass of beer, which he poured all over his head as he lifted the glass. After our initial outburst of laughter, we scattered to the four winds to avoid any further wrath from Dad. Not that it would have been too serious. His bark was worse than his bite.

Mothering My Own Children

You could say that a positive outcome of not having a mother was the blank canvas that I had when raising my own children. Without a blueprint for motherhood, I probably made many mistakes, but I truly believe that the Holy Spirit guided me.

"You look just like your mother," people used to tell me. How I lapped that up, so desperate for memories and loving the idea that I was like her. She had been part of a ballet corps as a young woman and so that is what I aspired to do. I only did it for a term at the age of about four because of moving home a lot in those early years and Dad didn't have the time or resources to enroll us in after school activities. Later, I satisfied my longings through my own children, hence sending my daughter to dance classes and my son to piano lessons. Thankfully, they both loved and pursued these hobbies into adulthood, because in all honesty I was just trying to give them what I never had, wanting to fulfil my own needs and desires through them.

I used to feel any rejection they experienced so keenly as though it was I who was being rejected. My daughter was once invited to an afternoon birthday party. All the little girls were invited to stay over for a sleepover except for two, one of whom was my daughter. She may not have minded but the feeling of rejection cut me deeply.

I probably was overzealous and protective and I also tried to be there for every school event, which my father hadn't been able to always do. I wanted to be available for them always, but perhaps this was smothering at times.

I have also had the privilege of being a spiritual mother to a young orphaned Ugandan man, Robert, who dropped into our lives when he was nineteen while on a three month tour of the UK to raise money for the Pearl of Africa Children's Choir. In the following years our family has supported him and grown to love and treat him as our son.

Mother Heart of the Father

I have a treasured photograph of my father when he was in the army wearing his officer's uniform and looking so handsome. It's one of my favourites: his officer's hat tilted over his forehead, broad smile, arms outstretched, white gloves in his hand as he walks across a lawn to greet his mother (Nana). His own father died when he was a boy during World War II from natural causes and so my father missed out on fathering throughout the latter part of his childhood. My grandmother filled the role of both parents as best she could.

When we come into a relationship with God, we can begin to experience both his father- and his mother-heart. One of the many names of God is El Shaddai.

According to Jeff A. Benner writing about El Shaddai for the Ancient Hebrew Research Center, most Bible translations translate the word *Shaddai* as "Almighty." He explains that the Hebrew word שדי *(shaddai)* also has the meaning of a "teat." The goat was a very common animal within the herds of the Hebrews. Goats produce milk from two teats dangling below the udder which is extracted by the goat kids by squeezing and sucking and provides all the necessary nourishment they need and without which, they would die. Just as the goat provides nourishment to its kids through the milk, God nourishes His children through His milk and provides all the necessities of life. This imagery can be seen in the following passage of Exodus 3:8:

"And I will come down to snatch them [Israel] from the hand of the Egyptians and to bring them up from that land to a good and wide land to a land flowing with milk and honey."

The word "Shadai" שדי *(teat)* is often coupled with the word "El" אל *(mighty, strong)*, creating the phrase אל שדי *(el shaddai)* literally meaning the "mighty teat."

Mr. Benner goes on to say, "The idea of God being characterised as having teats does not sit well in our Western culture. We are familiar with identifying with God as a father, but not as a mother.

The Hebrew word for mother is אם *(em)* or in the ancient pictographic script. The ox head meaning "strength" combined with the picture for "water" forms the word meaning "strong water." Animal's hides were placed in a pot of boiling water. As the hide boiled, a thick sticky substance formed at the surface of the water and was removed and used as glue, a binding liquid or "strong water." The mother of the family is the "one who binds the family together." God can be seen as the "glue" that holds the whole universe together."

"God is 'Shaddai,' because he is the nourisher, the strength giver, and so, in a secondary sense, the Satisfier, who pours himself into believing lives. As a fretful, unsatisfied babe, is not only strengthened and nourished from the mother's breast, but also is quieted, rested, and satisfied. So, El Shaddai is that name of God, which sets Him forth as the strength giver and satisfier of his people." (Michelle McClain-Walters)

The Holy Spirit, one of the Trinity alongside the Father and Jesus, can also be seen to express the tenderness of a mother. The Greek word used by Jesus to describe the Holy Spirit in John 14:26 is *paraclete*, meaning advocate, helper, comforter or one who consoles. I don't want to draw conclusions that consoling and comforting are feminine attributes, but mothers are the first to bond with their newborn child and provide necessary comfort and nourishment in their first few weeks.

Jesus himself, the express image of the Father, who only did what His father in heaven told Him, also had a nurturing, tender heart towards his own people when lamenting their rejection of Him,

"O Jerusalem, Jerusalem, the city that kills the prophets and stones God's messengers! How often I have wanted to gather your children together as a hen protects her chicks beneath her wings, but you wouldn't let me. (Luke 13:34, NLT)

Jesus was blessed to grow up with two fathers! He had a loving heavenly father and his earthly father, Joseph, who raised Him and taught Him his trade. Mary, His mother, nurtured and guided Him. Although He would have taught her much as the son of God, which she pondered in her heart. She had to experience the agony of watching Him die before her, and in the most horrific way. What a thing for a mother to have to bear.

Many have not received nurturing or bonding love, whether due to a lack of mothering or the tenderness of a father. Typically, until recent decades it was not acceptable for a man to be in touch with his feminine side. In war time Britain, boys grew up overnight and a culture existed of having a stiff upper lip; i.e. staying resolute and unemotional, especially in the face of adversity. Little children were to be seen and not heard, so the saying went, and boys especially should not cry. I think of poor Nigel going to boarding school, so young.

I believe a revolution has been taking place as men increasingly take on the parenting role in the home, some swapping places with their wives as homemaker and caregiver to the children. Men have been getting in touch with their own femininity and are bonding with their children in ways that they themselves may not have experienced when growing up. While not advocating the emasculation of men, some of the loveliest men I've met are those who are in touch with their feminine side.

My own father, as a single parent of six children, was caring and relational. On my first day of senior school, aged eleven, he put me on the bus to go to the station where I would take the train to my new grammar school and when I got to my destination he was already there, hovering, wanting to ensure that I had arrived safely. Even as adults, married with children, if we went away on holiday with our families, he wanted to know that we had arrived home safely afterwards. I always laugh when I think of Nicole who lives in France returning to visit Dad; her plane had barely landed at Heathrow Airport and she had stood up, reaching up to get her hand luggage from the overhead locker when she received a call on her mobile. It was Dad,

“Nicole, darling, your flight has landed.” He had been monitoring her journey, anxiously checking up on every leg. I am so grateful for the care and tenderness of my father and how he sought to meet our needs and care like a mother.

In the musical *Grease*, the protagonists Danny and Sandy have a holiday romance and alone with Sandy, Danny does not put on any airs or pretences. As soon as he’s back at Rydell High, this immediately comes into conflict with his reputation as cool, tough and “one of the gang,” when he discovers that Sandy has joined the school. He's so excited to see her on their first meeting at school after their holiday romance, until he suddenly remembers that all his friends are watching his every move. They have an expectation of how he is going to behave because of the image he has cultivated. So, the walls go up and he swaggers around, portraying a cool, nonchalant, macho demeanour which is alienating to Sandy who laments to him that he is not the Danny she knows and she certainly doesn't like the one she is now seeing! Until he is willing to get in touch with his real self and be genuine in public, their relationship is doomed. When he does that, Sandy also begins to come out of her shell and they begin to transform into their true identities, comfortable with being real with each other and those in their peer group. This has a positive knock-on effect. Too often our unfounded fears of how others will react to the ‘real me’ paralyse us. It begets the question, are you willing to present the real you to those around you or are you not being true to your identity?

Chapter 8
RECEIVING CHRIST

"I have come that they may have life, and have it to the full" (John 10:10, NIV).

So how do we discover who we are really meant to be? It is not about what we do, even when we have become very successful in our lives by the world's standards. Our exploits and achievements, our failures and unfulfilled dreams do not define us. What defines us is who we are at our core, who we were made to be; this takes off any pressure to perform or to get it right. I have discovered that it only comes from knowing our identity as children of God, the one who created us in his image. He knows all about us, how we tick, our likes and dislikes, what we will excel at, how to make the best of our lives because He made us. It begins by being accepted into God's family through a relationship with Jesus.

If you have already accepted Jesus as your Lord and Saviour, you can skip this first part; otherwise, please carefully read and consider His invitation to you. You will get so much more out of the rest of the book if you do.

If you have not yet accepted Jesus as your Lord and Saviour and would like to, please read the following and if you are ready to believe in Him say the prayer at the end:

Jesus said, "I have come that they may have life, and have it to the full" (John 10:10, NIV). Perhaps you have believed in the existence of God and His Son and have tried to live a good life, but have never consciously invited Him to be your Savior and Lord. No matter who you are or what you have done, at this very moment, you too can make the decision of a lifetime. Right now Jesus is knocking at the door of your heart.

We were all created to have a personal relationship with God who loves us, but because we all choose to go our own independent way; our relationship with God is broken. Our sin cuts us off from God so we cannot have a personal relationship with Him and experience His love. This applies to everyone, "For all have sinned and fall short of the glory of God" (Romans 3:23, NASB).

This cuts us off from God because He is holy (pure and sinless) and cannot tolerate sin. Romans 6:23, "The wages of sin is death"(NIV) this means spiritual separation from God. There is a chasm between us and Him which we cannot cross on our own as we are all sinners. But because God loves us so much he sent His son, Jesus to pay the penalty of our sins, "But God demonstrates His own love toward us, in that while we were yet sinners, Christ died for us" (Rom. 5:8, NASB).

The Bible teaches that Jesus is the only one way to bridge this chasm because he is the only one who has no sin in him. God sent His Son, Jesus Christ, to die on the cross in our place to pay the penalty for our sin. Jesus, who is fully God and fully man, came to earth to die in our place.

The Word became flesh and made his dwelling among us.
We have seen his glory, the glory of the one and only Son,
who came from the Father, full of grace and truth.
(John 1:14 NIV)

As a man, He overcame the temptations of sin that we face. He was completely without sin and so He is the only one who can pay the price for the sin of mankind.

Jesus said to him, "I am the way, and the truth, and the life;
no one comes to the Father, but through Me".
(John 14:6, NASV)

It is not enough just to know these truths. We must take the next step and "cross the bridge." We must individually receive Jesus Christ as Savior and Lord; then we can know God personally and experience His love.

"But as many as received Him, to them He gave the right to become children of God, even to those who believe in His name" (John 1:12, NASV).

"For God so loved the world, that He gave His only begotten Son, that whoever believes in Him should not perish, but have eternal life" (John 3:16, NASV).

"Now this is eternal life, that they know You,
the only true God and Jesus Christ
whom You have sent" (John 17:3 NIV).

God wants you to know Him

We receive Christ by personal invitation. Thus, receiving Him involves turning to God from self which is called repentance and trusting Christ to come into our lives to forgive our sins so that we can begin our personal relationship with Him. Just to know in our mind that Jesus Christ is the Son of God and that He died on the cross for our sins is not enough. Even the devil knows that. We receive Jesus Christ by faith, as an act of the will.

Jesus Christ is God's only cure for our sin. Through Him you can know God personally and experience His love.

Would you like to accept Jesus' invitation to life?

You can receive Jesus Christ right now by faith through prayer. Here is a suggested prayer which can help you express your trust in Jesus, too:

DEAR LORD JESUS, I WANT TO KNOW YOU PERSONALLY. THANK YOU FOR DYING ON THE CROSS FOR MY SINS AND FOR RISING FROM THE DEAD. I OPEN THE DOOR OF MY LIFE AND RECEIVE YOU AS MY SAVIOUR AND LORD. I TRUST YOU NOW TO FORGIVE MY SINS AND GIVE ME ETERNAL LIFE. PLEASE MAKE ME THE KIND OF PERSON YOU WANT ME TO BE.

On holiday in Portugal
Memories
Vanessa & Ashley on the ship
from Nigeria to England
c.1971
Stephanie, Romayne and Nicole
w/ Ashley at school

4 generations of women
David's side (his mother is on the right)
Nana & David's wedding day
7th August 1957
Dad in military hospital c.1955
Family
Mummy in Hongkong
1950's
Dad as a toddler
Nana, David, Aunty Wanda, Uncle Arthur at Stephanie's christening 1958
Grandmother Nana's house
Reading, Berkshire

Maria Fernanda (Nana) & David holding Stephanie at her christening Hong Kong 1958

Dad greeting his mother at Sandhurst Military Academy

Nana in the centre c. early 1950's

All 6 children 1968

Romayne, Nicole, Vanessa, Nigel & Stephanie In Nigeria w/ Abadu c.1966

Stephanie & Vanessa in Nigeria c.1965

Rose Garden

Vanessa & Ashley w/Nana in her rose garden c.1972

Vanessa spinning in her cousin's garden c.1970

Vanessa in the garden c.1974

Vanessa picking roses c.1973

Vanessa c. 1974

P

PART 3:

TOOLS FOR RESTORING AND LIVING OUT OUR IDENTITY

I want to share what I will call the 10 "B"s which have been instrumental in helping me find my identity. I am not a theologian or a psychologist and can only share from my own experience.

Chapter 9
BE-HOLD

Behold definition (Merriam Webster Dictionary

1. :to perceive through sight or apprehension: ***SEE***
2. :to gaze upon: ***OBSERVE.***

It was a pleasure to *behold* the beauty of the sunset.
The enormous crowd was a sight to *behold.*

According to Bob Lonac, "'Behold' is used 1,298 times in the King James version of the Bible. It is derived from the Greek word 'eido,' which has the literal translation of: be sure to see. Or as I like to think of it – don't miss this."

Until we gaze upon Jesus, we will never truly know who we are or what we are supposed to do with our lives. Why is that? Because we were made in His image, the image of our Creator, God, so when we see and know Him, we will know ourselves. As Bob Lomac says, "don't miss this!"

The first chapter of Genesis describes how God created the world and everything in it, including mankind: Genesis 1:26, "Then God said, 'Let us make man in our image, after our likeness'" (ESV). Genesis 2:7, "[...] then the

LORD God formed the man of dust from the ground and breathed into his nostrils the breath of life, and the man became a living creature" (ESV).

"For in him all things were created: things in heaven and on earth, visible and invisible, whether thrones or powers or rulers or authorities; all things have been created through him and for him"
(Colossians 1:16 NIV).

And we have a helper, for as we invite him into our hearts His Spirit comes to dwell in us, the spirit of the living God who reveals Jesus to us. 1 Corinthians 2:16 NIV, "Who has known the mind of the Lord so as to instruct him?" But we have the mind of Christ. The more we gaze upon Jesus, the more we are transformed into His likeness. This could be through reading the word as He is The Word and is revealed all through scripture.

The word is living and active and transforms us: Hebrews 4:12, "For we have the living Word of God, which is full of energy, like a two-mouthed sword. It will even penetrate to the very core of our being where soul and spirit, bone and marrow meet! It interprets and reveals the true thoughts and secret motives of our hearts" (TPT).

The word exposes to us anything that does not line up with His character. This is not to shame us, but to help change us and renew our minds so that we can live free, unencumbered from guilt, and condemnation. When Jesus looks at us, He never accuses us, but He does confront our sin and wants us to change our ways. Jesus, himself said that He did not come to condemn but to bring life.

Psalm 34:5 is one of my favourite bible verses:

"Those who look to him are radiant, and their faces will never be ashamed" (ESV).

Spending time with Jesus, praying, worshipping, reading the word, being in His presence with no agenda brings healing, restoration, and transformation. As we come into His presence with expectant, open hearts, and a willingness to change or do whatever He shows us, will transform us from glory to glory. This process of change can take place as we behold the Lord in other believers who carry His presence and who have spent much time with Him in the secret place of intimacy and reflect His nature. This can rub off on us as iron sharpens iron if we allow it.

"Perfection, wholeness, and health in every area manifest as you live consciously beholding Almighty God. He is the wisdom of the Ages. Jesus is the doorway that is open before you. Step in. Make the Lord's presence your dwelling place and the troubles of this world will grow strangely dim"

(Wright & Rodriguez, Day 46).

Have you ever been convicted, for example, when you have shared a snippet of gossip with a Christian friend? Kidding yourself that you are sharing so that the both of you can pray for or empathise with that person but really it's just you being a gossip, and yet the one you share with chooses not to engage with your ungodly behaviour? In that moment, you can choose to humble yourself, act like your friend, repenting to God for how you've actually seen yourself in contrast to your Christian friend's behaviour, or you can be disgruntled, offended that they didn't want to engage with your conversation, and walk away unchanged. Do you want to reflect Christ as you see Him in your friend or do you want to stay the same?

"Anyone who listens to the word but does not do what it says is like someone who looks at his face in a mirror and, after looking at himself, goes away and immediately forgets what he looks like" (James 1:23-24, NIV).

How do we begin to behold Him?

The answer is simply to invite Him into our hearts, just as I, sitting in the dark on my own during the night hours while breastfeeding my six-week old daughter, offered up a simple prayer to invite Him into my life. He was waiting for that moment, for in truth, He knew me before I was born. He created me and loved me even more than I loved the baby in my arms, which is hard to imagine for a mother of a newborn and was longing for me more than I did for Him. He puts that longing to know Him inside of us. I like to describe it that we are born with a heart shaped hole in us which we are always looking to fill but don't realise what it is we are searching for until we find Jesus.

Behold, I stand at the door and knock. If anyone hears My voice and opens the door, I will come in to him and dine with him, and he with Me. (Revelation 3:20 NKJV)

Remain in Me, and I (will remain) in you. (John 15:4 AMP)

Chapter 10
BE KNOWN

O LORD, you have examined my heart and know everything about me.
(Psalm 139:1 NLT)

Anyone who has ever designed or made anything will be an authority on how that thing functions. I have a Cartier watch and whenever it needs a service or breaks down, I send it to Cartier in London, because they know its intricate workings better than anyone. I put it in the hands of the experts and yield it to their knowledge and expertise. This is far greater than mine as I am just the wearer.

Likewise, we put ourselves in the hands of our maker who formed us. He knows how we were made, our purpose, which environment we thrive in, which environment is not good for us, and how to fix us when we are broken even better than we know ourselves. Because He made us and knows the good plans He has for our lives. He foresees the ups and the downs; He made us with all the character traits, giftings and strengths we need to equip us for success.

Psalm 139 tells us how completely He knows us because He planned us and formed us. He even knows us better than we know ourselves.

O LORD, you have examined my heart and know everything about me.
(Psalm 139:1 NLT)

(See Afterword on p.234 for the full Psalm)

There is a famous King in the Bible called Cyrus, King of Persia, who, although not a Jew, set the Jews free from their Babylonian captivity that had taken place decades before. Cyrus facilitated their return to the Promised Land and he became a notable figure in Jewish scripture as a saviour who helped them build the Second Temple in Jerusalem. It is of note that Cyrus was first mentioned in the Bible almost one hundred fifty years beforehand by the prophet Isaiah. Isaiah prophesied that Jerusalem would fall more than one hundred years before it happened and that Cyrus would allow the Jews to return after captivity in Babylon to rebuild it. Later, historians said that Cyrus read this prophecy and was so moved that he carried it out.

Isaiah 45 is titled, "Cyrus, God's Instrument:

Thus says the LORD to His anointed,
To Cyrus, whose right hand I have held—
To subdue nations before him
And loose the armour of kings,
To open before him the double doors,
So that the gates will not be shut:
I will go before you
And make the crooked places straight;

I will break in pieces the gates of bronze
And cut the bars of iron.
I will give you the treasures of darkness
And hidden riches of secret places,
That you may know that I, the LORD,
Who call you by your name,
Am the God of Israel.
For Jacob My servant's sake,
And Israel My elect,
I have even called you by your name;
I have named you, though you have not known Me.
I am the LORD, and there is no other;
There is no God besides Me.
I will gird you, though you have not known Me,
That they may know from the rising of the sun to its setting
That there is none besides Me.
I am the LORD, and there is no other;
I form the light and create darkness,
I make peace and create calamity;
I, the LORD, do all these things.' (NKJV)

God calls Cyrus by name, 150 years before he was born and tells him what he will accomplish; even though he has not known God, God *knew* him.

So often, especially in today's world, people's lives are plastered all over social media: photos are airbrushed, plastic surgery changes how we really look, and people create personas of themselves through the posts they share that are not their true representations because they want to be seen and known in a certain way. They don't want people to see the real them. They want to be known but not as they really are. The problem it creates is that you and I desperately try to emulate them but will never attain that as they aren't reflecting reality. So we become dissatisfied with ourselves: too fat, not pretty enough, not having a good time, not popular and so it goes on.

I think of the 1999 Romantic comedy film *Notting Hill* in which Julia Roberts plays Anna Scott, a famous film star who happens to walk into a London bookstore owned by William Thacker (Hugh Grant) whose humdrum existence is thrown into romantic turmoil as they fall in love but then struggle to reconcile their radically different lifestyles in the name of love.

Being famous with a media-made image that doesn't reflect who Anna really is and known for the wrong reasons becomes a huge burden for them both. Anna tells of having had face lifts and her fear of letting people know the real her:

Anna Scott: Rita Hayworth used to say, "They go to bed with Gilda; they wake up with me."

William: Who's Gilda?

Anna Scott: Her most famous part. Men went to bed with the dream; they didn't like it when they would wake up with the reality. Do you feel that way?

William: You are lovelier this morning than you have ever been.

Later, when Anna realises she loves William and wants to be with him despite their differences and her fame, she goes to his bookshop to tell him, but he thinks it won't work out:

William: I live in Notting Hill. You live in Beverly Hills. Everyone in the world knows who you are, my mother has trouble remembering my name.

Anna Scott: I'm also just a girl, standing in front of a boy, asking him to love her.

You see, Anna is just a girl wanting to be known and loved for who she is inside.

The one person who knows us better than anyone else, even better than we know ourselves, is God and He is also the one who loves us beyond measure.

When Jesus finds a way to make Himself known to us, that is the beginning of us finding our true self. When we start to see Him, to behold Him in all his beauty and loveliness we begin to change, becoming more like Him. In His presence we receive love, truth, forgiveness, affirmation, healing and so much more, because He is all those things and reveals His nature to us.

If we are faithless, He remains faithful; He cannot deny Himself.
(2 Timothy 2:13 NKJV)

The more we see him the more we reflect him and are changed into his likeness. That's where we find our identity.

It doesn't mean we become clones, but we become free to be who He designed us to be before the foundation of the world. We no longer try to be like others, we are no longer in competition because we discover that Jesus says we are complete in Him and there is nothing we can do to make Him love us more or love us less. There's nothing we can do to please Him except to accept his love.

"One of the major agendas of heaven right now is to wake us up to who we truly are in Him." Robert Hotchkin, Founder of Men on the Frontlines and Robert Hotchkin Ministries on the Live Your Best Life Podcast.

Chapter 11
BE LOVED

I am my beloved's, and his desire is for me (Song of Soloman 7:10 ESV)

We are created to be loved. How do I know that? Because the one who created us is Love. His nature is love and everything He does is out of love for us. Our response is to love him back. Mark Davidson, author of Becoming The Beloved disagrees with many Christians who believe we are saved to serve. As I shared earlier, our identity should not come from what we do in life. Mark sums it up this way: "The truth is - you and I already have great value to God, simply because he has chosen to love us. We are not "saved to serve". We were saved to know love!"

When the fairytale princesses Aurora and Cinderella were awakened to love by their prince, they took on a new identity as beloved, and were given new positions as bride and princess, which also gave them a position of authority as royalty in the kingdom. Their new self-perception and how others now saw them strengthened them in their identity.

There are different types of love: friendly, romantic, and empathetic. The love I believe is the right of every child is the unconditional love of God, known as agape love. The closest thing to such love is the love of our parents and from the moment we are imagined, even before conception, our parents love us. We are born helpless and it is our parents who meet our needs. Even our parents can love us conditionally but the unconditional love of God means there are no strings attached, there is nothing we can do to earn his love. We do not need to appease him because He is not angry with us. We need to reprogram our belief system which has been distorted by religion and our own experience to believe that He can be a cruel taskmaster and that we need to do well to earn His love and if we make mistakes, He will withdraw it.

We can put God's name in place of love in the famous love passage of the Bible, 1 Corinthians 13, because He is Love.

God is patient and kind. God is not jealous or boastful or proud or rude. God does not demand His own way. God is not irritable, and He keeps no record of being wronged. God does not rejoice about injustice but rejoices whenever the truth wins out. God never gives up, never loses faith, is always hopeful, and endures through every circumstance. (Paraphrased -NLT)

The apostle Paul, longing for the church to become fully united to the love of Christ, prayed.

"[...]that you, being rooted and established in love, 18 may have power, together with all the Lord's holy people, to grasp how wide and long and high and deep is the love of Christ, 19 and to know this love that surpasses knowledge –that you may be filled to the measure of all the fullness of God"
(Ephesians 3:17–19, NIV)

The greatest love story ever told is the story of God sacrificing His one and only son because He loved the world so much. It began in a garden. Our oldest ancestors, the very first parents on Earth, Adam and Eve, created by God, had the privilege of walking with Him in the garden every day. They were loved, provided for, and given dominion over the earth by God. They lived in the garden of Eden and had everything they could ever need. Yet, they were enticed into wanting the one thing God told them not to eat. They listened to the voice of Satan speaking through the serpent, obeyed him instead of their Heavenly Father by eating from the tree of the knowledge of good and evil. God put them out of the garden where they had walked and talked with Him daily in order to keep them away from the tree of life which was also in the garden. Having sinned, if they then ate from that tree, they would live forever but it would be a life in sin. Their physical approach to eternal life was hence completely cut off. God foresaw this and already had a plan of redemption to bring them back into relationship with Him. The penalty for their sin and that of all their descendants, which means you and me, is death, and so thousands of years later God sent His son as a sinless man to die in place of Adam and Eve's descendants (all of humanity) so that we would no longer have to live our lives separated from Him. We are therefore no longer separated from God if we will accept Jesus as our Lord and saviour. The only way is through Him. You see, God loved us so much that He gave his only son Jesus to die for our sins so that we could be accepted back into His family.

Jesus answered, "I am the way and the truth and the life.
No one comes to the Father except through me"
(John 14:6, NIV).

He came to make us one with the father and we can call him Abba, which is the intimate word for father in Hebrew. I remember arriving at a hotel on my first trip to Jerusalem and was overwhelmed by the sight of a little Jewish girl running across the foyer to her daddy, calling Abba, who lovingly swung her up into his arms. That is how our Father in heaven wants to be to us.

Moreover, Jesus, who did everything His father did when on earth said, "let the little children come to me."

God loves family. He created Adam and drew Eve out of him because He said Adam needed a companion. Then He told them to be fruitful and multiply. He wanted to establish all the families on Earth from their union.

Jesus is asked, "Teacher, which is the greatest commandment in the Law? "Jesus replied: "'Love the Lord your God with all your heart and with all your soul and with all your mind.' This is the first and greatest commandment. And the second is like it: 'Love your neighbour as yourself.' All the Law and the Prophets hang on these two commandments" (Matthew 22:36-40, NIV).

Bible teacher Kenneth Copeland, Believer's Voice of Victory, once shared a vision that he had of a curtain rod lying on the floor. On it were the words from the above scripture. All the promises of God and spiritual laws in the Bible hang first and foremost on the law of love. To hang the curtains, we must first hang the rod! In other words, to fully participate in and receive all of God's promises we need to know we are fully and unconditionally loved. That means we are accepted as we are. There is nothing we can do to please Him as He already delights in us.

Because we live in an imperfect world most of us don't experience unconditional love and yet have an inner longing for more from life, that, unless filled, will leave us feeling incomplete. Most people do not even know they are missing something let alone love and they look in all the wrong places for fulfilment in life or they search for love from other wounded souls, which further damages their life experience.

As discussed in the chapter on mothers, ideally, our first experience of intimate love is the experience of family love. Apart from the love of God, the love of a father and mother is the most intimate kind of love we will ever know outside of a sexually intimate relationship. Experiencing love is foundational in forming our identity. I believe that the more we experience love, the closer we feel to the heart of God. We become His beloved, dearly loved and highly valued.

In *Becoming the Beloved: The End-Time Bride of Christ*, the author Mark Davidson shared his own personal struggle about learning his true identity as the beloved of God as, despite the knowledge that God loved him, he never felt loved by God but just tolerated, until God began to reveal to him his own true identity as his beloved.

According to Mark Davidson, we do not need to strive to become the beloved of God by good works. We become the beloved by simply receiving the love he offers us freely. Christ called us and declared us to be his bride, and that alone became the validation of our worth. We have done nothing to deserve it. God has chosen to love us and the only choice He has left for us to make is whether or not we will receive the gift of His love. The genesis of our becoming the beloved is found in simple longing. The Song of Solomon, a dialogue between two lovers, which has been described as the love between Christ and the human soul, begins with a Shulamite expressing her desire to be in a deeper relationship with the King and ends with her becoming the bride in divine union with the bridegroom King.

"Knowing Christ in his identity, as my bride groom, granted me a sense of my own true identity as well, I came to understand that being his bride had nothing to do with my gender or marital status. Being His bride is a state of heart." (Mark Davidson)

Some of My Love Story

Spinning on the lawn in my cousin's front garden, arms outstretched, face towards the sun, beginning to feel giddy until I stagger, then steady myself before tumbling to the ground– a moment of joy. You're so pretty in your new outfit, my aunty croons. I lap up the attention. There were similar incidents throughout my childhood, dots on a child's "join the dots" picture. I would carefully run the pencil from one to the next without lifting it from the paper, then poised over the dot I would press the lead down, mark it, store it in my stash of feel good memories. Oh no, I've gone the wrong way, reverse, rub out, start again. As I write this, I decide that if this were a painting it would be titled *Times of Love and Affirmation.*

It's present day again and I've got up early to sit with the Lord, my quiet time I call it. I put on some instrumental music and watch the moon peep out from the cloud over the sea through my conservatory window, casting a translucent glow over the sea, shimmering for a brief moment before the clouds swallow her up. In my imagination, I enter into the deep water, slowly, carefully, until my head is immersed. I am surprised by the memories that surface and linger, a gentle ebb and flow which causes tears to well from deep within: that little girl spinning in the garden, dancing around the sitting room with Aunty Pamela, and a visit from Aunty Terry with a gift, the kind air hostess who brought me a mango. I am reminded that even at the bottom of the Dead Sea, a salt lake in the desert of Southern Israel at the lowest point on Earth, they say there are fresh water springs. Those sporadic springs in my life were like wells of refreshing which I drank from thirstily.

When I first received Jesus into my life, I felt the peace of God very strongly but the honeymoon period, as I call it, began to wane. The Bible tells us we have to work out our salvation and get our minds renewed. Because our hearts can be broken there can be parts that we've compartmentalised and locked away to protect those parts and it is an ongoing process to let God's love seep into every area of our heart to make us whole. He is so tender and honours our hearts. He does it bit by bit, like taking the layers off an onion one at a time and I love that analogy because it often comes with tears.

I was like an onion with many layers. I had buried my feelings so deeply that I literally never cried and as God started to open up my heart to receive his love, those tears that were deep within me started to come up to the surface every time I was in the presence of God, at church or with other believers. I used to go to my local church where the vicar thought that I was a needy, emotional woman and he didn't know how to cope with me. He would call his wife to come quickly whenever I knocked on the door of the vicarage so he could make a hasty retreat.

One day I remember pondering the first commandment, "Love the Lord your God with all your heart and love your neighbour as yourself." I told God, "I don't know how to love. You're going to have to teach me." The answer came in an unexpected way by Him wooing *me* and demonstrating his love for *me*. Much of this was through the kindness of others. I had to learn to receive that kindness and especially the love from mother figures who began to come into my life more powerfully. It was actually very hard to start receiving because not only was I deft at putting up walls but I would also deflect attention from myself to others, soundly batting it away so I could protect my heart. Meeting someone I would steer the conversation, focusing it all on them without them noticing. It's been a very slow process but I've learned to feel safer and comfortable in allowing people to get close to me and to show love and kindness to me.

In the early days of my walk with Jesus, I asked Him why he hadn't just poured His love into me when I got saved. In answer He gave me a picture of a tiny seedling and said that was me when I received Him as Lord and Saviour. He showed me that the seedling had no roots and was growing in conditions similar to a dry sandpit without organic matter or moisture, because as yet I hadn't had any teaching from the Word of God, or revelation Truth or experience of Holy Spirit. Hence He only poured a little water at a time on the seedling, feeding it bit by bit with the word, daily nourishing me with revelation, wisdom, truth, and experiences of His love through the Holy Spirit and through those around me. It was like feeding a starving man who hasn't had proper nourishment for a long time. If you give them a large meal full of nutrients, they will be sick. Slowly, as my capacity to receive expanded, the plant grew. Moreover, had God poured out his love on me all at once, the little seedling would have just been washed away like a tree in a deluge or a house in a tsunami.

His promise to me and to you:

And hope does not put us to shame, because God's love has been poured out into our hearts through the Holy Spirit, who has been given to us. (Romans 5:5 NIV)

Chapter 12
BE YOU

Who am I that the highest king would welcome me?
I was lost but He brought me in Oh His love for me
In my Father's house there's a place for me
I am a child of God, Yes I am.
Lyrics by Hillsong Worship

Earlier, we discussed how personal identity refers to the unique ways that we define ourselves. How we see ourselves is going to radically change once we get saved and discover our relationship with Jesus, His love for us and how we fit into the family of God. When we first invite Jesus into our hearts, we begin to discover that our identity comes from being in Him. The Bible tells us that in Him we live and move and have our being. His spirit lives in us now, actively working in our souls and reviving our spirits. The Spirit gives us understanding of the Word, convicts of sin, and makes us holy. The Spirit equips us with gifts for ministry and sends us out into every sphere of life. The Spirit intercedes for us and bears witness with our spirit that we are the children of God.

Our identity in Christ is not based on education, economic worth, or social status, but our relationship with Him. As our relationship with Jesus develops and we start to believe all He says about us in His word, we become more confident about who we are.

I remember giving a talk once at church. I got a tin of beef stew, replaced its label with one for dog food and invited a brave young soul to come up and eat some. We opened the can in front of everyone. He had no idea that it wasn't dog food, but he was willing to try it. He took a bite and declared that it was quite palatable but everyone else was watching in disgust and horror because of the label they saw on the outside of the tin. So often we're not what the tin says we are and we have labels that we and others put on ourselves. We may do this for our own protection to keep people away from hurting us as we don't want them to know the real us. Other times people judge us by what they see on the outside, they make assumptions about us and label us. Whoever said "sticks and stones may hurt my bones but names will never hurt me," was sorely misguided! Let's rip the labels off and be real.

Discovering who we are through what the Bible says about us is wonderfully affirming but since we are uniquely made, God also wants to speak into our lives personally. We can ask Him, "W*ho do you say I am*?"

Some names He gives us are for the whole body of Christ, such as, child of God, new creation, the bride, God's workmanship. I like what Dan McCollam, co-founder of Bethel School of the Prophets said when speaking during a training in 100X *(a group for Kingdom Entrepreneurship)* "The written word gives your last name, the prophetic word your first. In other words, we can learn from the bible all about who we are, our rights, privileges, and blessings, which are for all believers." But God also knows each one of us by name and wants to speak into our identity through the prophetic word, and through revelation from the Holy spirit to encourage, edify and comfort.

I once asked Him, *who do you say I am?* He answered me, "I am my beloved's and my beloved is mine." That gave me such security that He dearly loved me in a season when I needed to know that. He may say something else to you, and He may give you a different name depending on your season. God Himself has many names, which reveal the different facets of His character that He reveals at different times in our lives. As we discover Him as healer, provider, shepherd, our peace, our righteousness and so many more (I would recommend a study on the names of God) we become transformed as we take on more of His nature.

In the Bible, we learn God even changed people's names, such as Abram to Abraham to confirm His covenant promise to him, and names were given to describe personality and character traits. Hence, when someone was transformed by God, He sometimes gave them a new name to seal it.

Jacob, whose name means *supplanter / deceiver* became *Israel* which means "wrestles with God" and "triumphant with God."

Just as Anna Scott came to the conclusion, "I am just a girl," so we too are called to simply *be.* After all, we are called human beings, not human doings! In today's fast paced world, where we are constantly on the go, surfing the internet and everything around us, we have lost the art of just being. The scripture tells us in Psalm 46 to be still and know God. Being still can be very difficult, not just in terms of sitting down for ten minutes, but in letting go of all the things we do which distract us, waste our time, and keep us so busy that we cannot get in touch with our true selves. It can be very uncomfortable when we first allow ourselves to be stripped away from the things we do to define ourselves. We become more connected with our thoughts and feelings and that can be uncomfortable. But it begins to give us the space to reflect more, and to allow God to heal any pains or trauma that we have blocked out by keeping busy and distracted, living on the surface.

"Come to me, all you who are weary and burdened, and I will give you rest. Take my yoke upon you and learn from me, for I am gentle and humble in heart, and you will find rest for your souls. For my yoke is easy and my burden is light." (Matthew 11:28-30 NIV)

God wants us to rest from toiling but to do so we need the courage to come face to face with ourselves as we learn to be still in our souls. As we allow Him in, He will bring revelation light and truth that will heal and restore us and we will discover who we are.

Chapter 13
BE AUTHENTIC

"Just as no two faces are exactly alike, so every heart is different."
(Proverbs 27:19 TPT)

"For we are His workmanship, created in Christ Jesus for good works, which God prepared beforehand that we should walk in them." (Eph 2:10 NKJV)

We can begin to live in the unique identity He has created for us. Even identical twins have different fingerprints, personalities, experiences and spirits. Some translations use the word *handiwork* or *masterpiece* to describe how God has perfectly created each one of us. The world tries to give us labels according to our job, class, generation, sexual orientation, our music, interests, politics, and the list goes on. We accept these, box ourselves and others in to define who we are and what we should and shouldn't do. Some of us like to hide behind these labels and find comfort and safety in the groups we identify with; but we will never be fully satisfied if we never discover who God created us to be.

We need to ask our Creator, what do you say about me? How have you made me uniquely different from others? God tells us we are unique, perfectly made for what He has planned for us to do with our lives. We need to trust Him in this and know that we are made just right for the perfect plan He has for us.

God knows every stage of our lives and so He plans us in advance for them. He knew the personality we would need to carry out His purpose in our lives, a role which no one else could fill. He even knew what bodies we would need, which family to be raised in, and nothing is a mistake.

When we are doing what we've been called to do, we will discover God has given us all we need to do it and we'll feel joy and satisfaction. It will be unique to us, so when we can learn to not copy others but to trust God, rest in Him and be ourselves, then we'll feel so much freer. We are a new creation and we are good.

The devil is a copycat and he doesn't want us to fulfil our destiny. He tried to be like God and got Adam and Eve to do the same. He wants us to copy each other and tries to convince us that we need to be like others, making us insecure– jealous even.

Don't apologise about who you are and what you love. Don't let go of your dreams, even if others don't understand you. Perhaps your parents exasperatedly told you that you're always so concerned that people do the right thing, or you're always dreaming, for example, and you took these as criticisms and thought you had better not be that way. Maybe that *is* how God made you.

I have spent much of my life apologising about myself, trying to fit, and fearing what others thought about me. This caused me a lot of pain later as I habitually formed unhealthy relationships from not being honest about how I felt, so the other person's behaviour would end up hurting me or stepping over my boundaries, which in the end left me feeling angry and powerless. I felt that I was becoming invisible as I chose to speak less and in fact, became fearful to speak out. When I did, the clamour in my head of accusation, telling me I shouldn't have spoken, that what I said had no value, that I had upset people, and so on, led me into a downward spiral of depression and anxiety.

It wasn't other people's fault as I hadn't been honest with them in the first place and they didn't know how I truly felt. I went through a season, not so long ago, where God showed me where I wasn't being honest and I had to rectify that in certain relationships. Sometimes you will lose that friendship because the other person wants you to stay the same or they want to remain the assertive and dominant one. Such relationships are not worth keeping.

"O my dove, [here] in the clefts in the rock, In the sheltered and secret place of the steep pathway, Let me see your face, Let me hear your voice; For your voice is sweet, And your face is lovely."
(Song of Solomon 2:14 AMP)

As I became more in touch with who I am, emotions and reactions started to stir in me that had been dormant. This was quite a difficult thing to deal with. Coming out of a long season of squashing my own personality, suppressing my emotions and not sharing my views thinking they didn't matter to suddenly finding myself reacting angrily, speaking my views and letting them pour out like a tirade. I would then beat myself up afterwards. This was all okay and part of the process of being transformed as I became more in touch with who I am and learning my opinion does matter.

I liken it to when your foot or arm has "gone to sleep". It feels dead and numb after you've lain on it at night and as the blood starts to rush back in it can be excruciating as you get pins and needles and that part of you comes back into circulation.

Your thoughts and actions may need refining and directing too as you become more authentic. The process can seem ugly, such as the misplaced passion that rose up in Moses to protect his people which led him to kill the Egyptian for badly treating one of them, or when Joseph told his older brothers his dreams of them bowing down to him; which no doubt infuriated them. Sometimes everything seems messy before it becomes clear.

Be transformed by the renewing of your mind into the image of Christ, the only one in whose image we were created to be. Let us make man in our likeness, the Creator said. He is beautiful and multifaceted; He does not limit us but transforms us into the unique person He has called us to be. We will find true fulfilment when we are truly free to be ourselves. We need to be real and authentic.

Ask God:

Who have you created me to be?
What are the personality traits you gave me?

Authenticity and the Church

I just want to share a little of my younger sister Ashley's faith journey and her search for authenticity. At a difficult time in her life she joined her local church in search of support and fellowship. She also seriously wanted to explore her faith and finally resolve her scepticism about God's existence.

Within the church, she found the community and loving support she was looking for as she threw herself in with gusto, not being one to do things by halves, but was unable to ever feel sincere about her faith. She wanted the faith others seemed to have around her, but the liturgy, observances and behaviours never rang true with her; and so with time, as her need for support and community waned, Ashley drifted away from church and from a potential relationship with God.

I find it sad, disheartening and not untypical, that churches are unable to hold on to those who are truly seeking. Serving in Sunday school or on the worship team may be fun and build community, but in the end, it doesn't satisfy our inner longing. That can only be experienced in a loving relationship with God and from an authenticity to be ourselves that doesn't require us to follow church programs to be qualified.

Even the church is infiltrated with the need to perform to find identity, just like every other sector of society.

Chapter 14
BE CHANGED

And do not be conformed to this world but be transformed by the renewing of your mind, that you may prove what is that good and acceptable and perfect will of God. (Romans 12:2 NKJV)

Many of us regret our past, the mistakes we have made, the hurts and traumas we have experienced, and the person we have become because of the choices we have made just because life is hard. If we are old, we think it is too late to start again.

God is in the restoration business and as soon as we are born again, we become new creations, our slate is literally wiped clean. All of our sins are forgiven, in fact forgotten by God. You may bring them up, but He won't remember them. When I say all, it means He has even forgiven you of the sins you haven't committed yet. That isn't a licence to carry on sinning though! If we consciously mess up, He has given us the gift of repentance which means that as we genuinely say sorry to God, He forgives us instantly. Why? Because Jesus took all of our sin on the cross over two thousand years ago.

Even though we have been forgiven, we can still carry the emotional pain from our unhealed hurts, unresolved issues and unmet needs. God can change all of that. As we spend time with Him and get revelation from His word, our minds get renewed.

We can't change what happened to us, but we can learn to understand our experiences from God's perspective. What we perceive as reality can be replaced with His truth, such as if we were always left to fend for ourselves and so believe that since no one is there for us, we are going to have to learn to cope on our own. That is, until we get the truth that God will never leave us nor forsake us and that He will supply all of our needs.

We may have been told that we will never amount to anything and so we don't do much with our lives, as we don't expect that we will succeed. God says that He knows the plans He has for us and they are good and that we can do all things through Christ.

Can you see how you can rewrite the narrative of your own story? As I began to write this book and look at my story, Jesus would show me the lies I had believed at various stages of my life because of what I had experienced. Then, He was able to bring His truth to the situation with the help of the scriptures because the Bible contains the infallible word of God and is our instruction manual for right living.

Often, it will mean I need to forgive those who have hurt me, whether it was intentional or not, whether they are alive or dead, I can release them to Jesus and let Him deal with them if need be. We may need to repent of things He shows us we have done. I don't just mean obvious things like stealing or coveting. One of the most subtle ways the devil traps us in sin is through offence. It is so easy to get offended by what someone has said or done, and we need to release that person from the hook of offence and check our hearts are loving and forgiving.

We need to be willing to let God search our hearts daily.

He is a gentleman and will never violate your personal space. If you ask, He will help you heal from your past. Remember, He will always speak with the voice of love. If you feel accused or that God is being angry with you, then it is not Him.

"Jesus said, 'My sheep hear my voice; I know them, and they follow me'" (John 10:27 NIV).

If you have asked Jesus into your life you will learn to recognise His voice of love and reject the other dialogue in your head, be it your own or that of the devil who always accuses.

Chapter 15
BE-LONG

...and you belong to Christ; and Christ belongs to God.
(1 Corinthians 3:23 NLT)

"I pray for them. I do not pray for the world but for those whom You have given Me, for they are Yours"
(John 17:9 NKJV)

When we are born again into the Kingdom of God, we are no longer of this world but belong to God. We are new creations. You have probably heard it said that we are spirit, that we have a soul and that we live in a body. An astronaut suit gives the ability to survive in space. Likewise, our earthly body is the suit we wear to enable us to be on the earth which is our temporary dwelling.

When Jesus was praying to the father for His disciples in John 17:15-16 NKJV, he said "I do not pray that You should take them out of the world, but that You should keep them from the evil one. They are not of the world, just as I am not of the world".

When we are born again, we are adopted into the family of God, becoming His children. We now belong to Him. There are many verses in the Bible about belonging to God.

Chapter 16
BE-COMING
Becoming A Daughter

But to all who believed him and accepted him, he gave the right to become children of God. They are reborn—not with a physical birth resulting from human passion or plan, but a birth that comes from God. (John 1:12-13, NLT)

"I will be a Father to you, and you will be my sons and daughters, says the Lord Almighty." (2 Corinthians 6:18, NIV)

I used to think of God as distant and strict; sitting somewhere up in heaven, on his throne ready to tell me off whenever I did the wrong thing. It seemed to me I did the wrong thing often. I have memories of creeping down the stairs most nights when I was about eight or nine, finding Dad and telling him that I was sorry, he saying it was ok. Then, me padding back up the stairs barefoot, feeling a bit better for our exchange of words, feet icy cold from the flagstones in the hallway. Yet, I can't even remember why I was apologising. There was just always this nagging feeling of not doing the right thing coupled with the fear of getting into trouble. For years, after being saved, I would see God on His throne, unapproachable and ready to judge me. It has taken a relationship with Jesus, and a renewing of my mind by the Holy Spirit through the Word to reveal the true loving heart of the Father to me. That is why this chapter is titled "Becoming A Daughter." I guess for some, the revelation of God's unconditional love as our Father can be instant, but for most of us it takes time to build trust and confidence in Him; especially as one who will keep us safe and provide for us, who is never angry and who wants us to run to Him and not from Him when we do wrong. To know that He is always ready to scoop us up, like little children. The more we experience this, the more we will trust Him.

If you have had a poor relationship with your own father, no father at all, have been abused, not protected, or provided for by father figures in your life, then it is likely that you will not see God as a loving father. He wants to heal the pain of your past so you can trust Him and often the best way is to come to Jesus first. Jesus tells us that when you have seen Him, you have seen the Father. Jesus is the image of the invisible God. He is a safe place to start. I want to encourage you to ask Jesus how you see the Father and ask Him to help you in the areas where you have believed lies about Him. There is so much the Father wants to restore to you. He delights in giving His children good things and He wants you to succeed in your life, just like any good parent. Remember, He is proud of you, even if you don't do anything notable, and even if you make mistakes. He always loves you. He cannot help that as that is His nature.

See what great love the Father has lavished on us,
that we should be called children of God! (1 John 3:1 NIV)

As a father has compassion on his children, so the Lord has compassion on those who fear him. This is not the kind of fear of punishment for sin, but a deep reverence for and awareness of God. (Psalm 103:13 NIV)

There is no fear in love. But perfect love drives out fear,
because fear has to do with punishment. The one who fears
is not made perfect in love. (1 John 4:18 NIV)

Let Jesus and the Father love you until all your fear of punishment has gone.

Be-coming a Citizen of Heaven

But [we are different, because] our citizenship is in heaven.
And from there we eagerly await [the coming of] the Saviour,
the Lord Jesus Christ; (Philippians. 3:20 AMP)

We become a citizen of the Kingdom of God, a son and daughter of God and a co-heir with Christ when we are born again. This means we receive all the benefits of a son/daughter, but we also willingly live our life by His commands and guide our life by the constitution of God's kingdom, which is the Word of God. As a Kingdom citizen, we align with God's lordship by aligning our life with what God has said in His word.

We are physically present in the world but not part of its values. There is another way we follow now, which the world doesn't understand; such as forgiving others, not taking offence, sowing, and not holding onto material things as our treasures are in heaven. This can be difficult, if we are not secure in our identity as sons and daughters of God. If we try to hold onto earthly values and do what the world does and expects of us, it can magnify our feeling of being different in a negative way. We do not fit and we will never fit, but that's ok, when we know who and whose we are and trust in God's promises and provision.

The Kingdom of God does not operate like earth. In fact, everything seems turned on its head! When people hurt us, we turn the other cheek, we give instead of taking from others, we love them and do not retaliate when they hate us. From Jesus' short time on earth we can learn much on how to live our lives. Jesus, although God, gave up his rights to be God. He came to serve us and gave His life as a ransom for many. For the joy set before him (humankind) He endured the cross. He is our role model and He invites us to show our love for Him by doing what He does, by loving and serving others. We demonstrate our love for Him when we minister to people, and love and serve them as he would, seeing them as He sees them.

Being a citizen of Heaven also means that we are God's ambassadors on Earth and are afforded all the protection and rights of the Kingdom. There is also the expectation of behaviour as we represent the King. We are loyal to Him. We also abide by the laws and submit to the ruling authorities placed over us on earth as all authority has been put there by God. Unless it compromises our faith, we seek to follow the rules around us, just as Jesus told

Peter to pay the temple tax even though Jesus is God and could have exercised His rights.

Being an ambassador of Heaven can be difficult when our peers are pressuring us and when temptation arises to act the way the world does. Jesus will not let us be tempted beyond what we can endure. If we cry to Him for help, He will be there. He will never forsake us, and He willingly forgives us when we fall short and repent.

Be-coming the Bride

Let us rejoice and be glad and give Him glory. For the wedding of the Lamb has come, and His bride has made herself ready (Revelation 19:7 NIV)

You may have heard people jokingly say, "Jesus, is coming; look busy."

Maybe they are hoping He won't notice the things they are ashamed of in their lives or maybe they don't know Him at all, don't like who they think He is and want to have nothing to do with Him. The truth is that He is coming back for a spotless bride, those who know and love Him, and there is going to be a great wedding and celebration in Heaven on that day.

The Ancient Jewish Wedding

It would be appropriate to share here the striking similarities between a traditional ancient Jewish wedding and the Biblical references to Jesus and the bride.

This ancient Jewish ritual prophetically points to the coming of the Messiah and the great celebration of the marriage supper of the Lamb.

There are three distinct parts to the ancient Jewish wedding: shiddukhin (mutual commitment), erusin (engagement), and nissuin (marriage).

Shiddukhin refers to the preliminary arrangements prior to the legal betrothal. The father of the groom often selected a bride (kallah) for his son, as did Abraham for his son Isaac (Genesis 24:1-4) and as Father God did when He sent his Son, Jesus Christ to Earth to rescue mankind.

In ancient times, marriage was looked upon as more of an alliance for reasons of survival or practicality, and the concept of romantic love was secondary, if considered at all. Romantic love grew over time. I find this element fascinating as when I received Jesus, I didn't know how to receive or give love and it too has grown over time in my heart.

The consent of the bride-to-be was considered important. Rebecca, for example, was asked if she agreed to go back with Abraham's servant to marry Abraham's son, Isaac. She went willingly (Genesis 24:57–59).

Traditionally, in preparation for the betrothal ceremony, the bride (kallah) and groom (chatan) are separately immersed in water in a ritual called the mikvah, which is symbolic of spiritual cleansing.

In Matthew 3:13–17, we read that Yeshua has already been immersed (baptised) by John in the Jordan River. As the bride-to-be, we are also asked to be immersed.

"Whoever believes and is baptised will be saved, but whoever does not believe will be condemned" (Mark 16:16, NIV).

Erusin: The Betrothal

"He who finds a wife finds what is good and receives favour from the Lord" (Proverbs 18:22, NIV).

After the immersion, the couple entered the huppah (marriage canopy) which is symbolic of a new household being planned, to establish a binding contract. Here, the groom would give the bride money or a valuable object such as a ring, and a cup of wine was customarily shared to seal their covenant vows. In this public ceremony under the huppah, the couple entered into the betrothal period, which typically lasted for about a year. Although they were considered married, they did not live together or engage in sexual relations. During the erusin period, the groom was to prepare a place for his bride, while the bride focused on her personal preparations: wedding garments, lamps, etc., just as we the church prepare ourselves for Jesus' return. Although the bride knew to expect her groom after about a year, she did not know the exact day or hour. He could come earlier. It was the father of the groom who gave final approval for him to return to collect his bride.

Regarding the second coming of Jesus:

"But about that day or hour no one knows, not even the angels in heaven, nor the Son, but only the Father" (Matt. 24:36 NIV).

For that reason, the bride kept her oil lamps ready at all times, just in case the groom came in the night, sounding the shofar (ram's horn) to lead the bridal procession to the home he had prepared for her. In the Parable of the Ten Virgins in Matthew chapter 25, Jesus likened the Kingdom of Heaven to this special period of erusin, when the groom comes for his bride, "At midnight the cry rang out: 'Here's the bridegroom! Come out to meet him!' Then all the virgins woke up and trimmed their lamps." Matt 25:6 NIV. So too, today, as we await Jesus' return, we should be careful to remain alert and prepared for His coming.

Nissuin: The Marriage

When everything is ready, I will come and get you,
so that you will always be with me where I am."
(John 14:3, NLT)

The final step in the Jewish wedding tradition is called nissuin (to take), a word that comes from naso, which means to lift up.

It was routine in Jesus' day for kiddushin and nisuin to be separated by as much as a year. During that time the bridegroom would set up the marital home. Similarly, after sealing the covenant with the Church, Jesus ascended to His Father's home to prepare a dwelling place for His bride. Just prior to

His death, Jesus told His disciples, "There is more than enough room in my Father's home. If this were not so, would I have told you that I am going to prepare a place for you?" John 14:2, NLT

According to Jewish marriage law, when the time came for nisuin, the groom would return for his bride accompanied by male escorts. The exact time of his arrival was not usually known in advance (see Matthew 25:1–15). The groom's arrival was announced with a shout. The church's bridegroom has been separated from His Bride now for nearly 2,000 years, and one day He will come for her and snatch her from the Earth to meet Him in the air (1 Thessalonians 4:17). We don't know when exactly this will happen; we must be ready and remain faithful (Mark 13:33). Jesus will be accompanied by an angelic escort, preceded by a shout, when He returns for the Church (1 Thessalonians 4:16).

After being whisked from her home, the Jewish bride remained hidden at the groom's father's house for seven days. Similarly, the church will remain "hidden" for a period of seven years, during the prophesied tribulation. After the seven days, the Jewish bride left the bridal chamber unveiled; likewise, after seven years the church will return to Earth with Christ, in full view of all (Colossians 3:4).

The day of the return of the Messiah for His Bride is soon approaching. Although, we know approximately the time of His return from the signs of the times, "the day of the Lord will come like a thief in the night." 1 Thess 5:2, ESV

The Bride (Believers in Jesus) should be living consecrated lives, keeping themselves pure and holy in preparation for the Nissuin and the Wedding Feast of the Lamb, when the Groom comes with the blast of the shofar (1 Thessalonians 4: 16) to bring His Bride home.

The Preparation of the Bride

Although God is never mentioned in the book of Esther, it portrays a beautiful picture of the preparation of the bride before she is presented to the king. She spent six months having oil of myrrh treatments and six months of spices and cosmetic treatment prior to being presented to him. Esther was taken to King Ahasuerus, into his royal palace, in the tenth month, which is the month of Tebeth, in the seventh year of his reign. Esther 2:17NKJV "The king loved Esther more than all the other women, so Esther obtained grace and favour in his sight more than all the virgins; so he set the royal crown upon her head and made her queen instead of Vashti. Then the king made a great feast, the Feast of Esther, for all his officials and servants; and he proclaimed a holiday in the provinces and gave gifts according to the generosity of a king." When she courageously went before him uncommanded on pain of death, because she pleased him so much and found favour with him, he said he would grant her any request, up to half his kingdom. On telling him she was a Jew and asking him to save her people from the wicked Haman and his plot to exterminate the Jews, he granted her request.

We too are being prepared like Esther for our bridegroom king. We are created to become the bride of Christ which is our true identity. I have been blessed to have had visions and pictures over the years of how God is redeeming and restoring the Bride; how He is awakening her because she is asleep and doesn't know her identity. Recall the story of Aurora in *Sleeping Beauty*. God wants to give you your identity as the *beloved Bride* and He is inviting you to receive Him as the Bridegroom, Matt. 2:19-20, NKJV.

That would explain the longings I had as a new believer, to sit at His feet, to minister to Him and the longing I had to be loved. I remember this culminating some years later when one Sunday morning I announced to my church that I wanted time out from serving to get to know Jesus again. Despite being part of only a small congregation, it had been a busy season of being involved in all sorts of church programs and my relationship with the Lord had waned. I wasn't putting him first and wanted, no, needed to get back to those intimate times of connection when I wasn't looking for the next thing, He wanted me to share or give to others; but to just hear and know Him for myself. Like the wise virgins, I wanted to be prepared for His coming with oil in my lamp. I remember standing at the front of the church and telling the people I was going to have time out and many of them stared blankly at me as if they didn't understand what I was talking about. One lady, as well meaning as she was, told me that I was a mess. Does that what longing for Jesus look like to others?

We need to remember that we do not get our identity as his beloved by what we do. Indeed, Jesus himself said, "Not everyone who says to Me, 'Lord, Lord,' shall enter the kingdom of heaven, but he who does the will of My Father in heaven. Many will say to Me in that day, 'Lord, Lord, have we not prophesied in Your name, cast out demons in Your name, and done many wonders in Your name?' And then I will declare to them, 'I never knew you; depart from Me, you who practise lawlessness!'" (Matt. 7:21-23, NKJV)

Our works will not get us into Heaven. One vision the Lord has given me, several times over the years, is a picture of me holding some beautiful, precious jewels tightly in my hand and the Lord is asking me to release them. They may look good, and it is commendable to serve as He gives us gifts to do that; but when they become more important to us than our relationship to Him, He may ask us to let them go. In my vision, I enter into the bedchamber and lay my head on the pillow. This may seem offensive to some, but it is a picture of rest and intimacy with the Lord.

In *Becoming the Beloved*, Mark Davidson believes that there are two types of people awaiting Jesus' return - servants and brides. Those who serve, work hard and are treated as servants but they will not be invited into the wedding chamber. The bride, he says, is composed of those who know and experience Christ as their bridegroom. It is all about their relationship. They are not so concerned with service, although when you know and receive God's love you cannot help but want to bring others into the knowledge of it and offer acts of loving service.

It is not for me to say who Jesus will leave outside the door when He comes for His bride. All I know is that I have a yearning in my heart for Him and I want to tell you that if you feel the same way, that you are not weird. It is ok to sit at His feet, even if others don't understand you. He sees and delights in your adoration of Him and you will not be disappointed.

In one of my favourite Bible stories, Jesus is lavished with perfume by Mary before He goes to the cross. Judas, who would betray Him very shortly after that and who looked after the coffers, was more concerned that the money from the costly perfume should have been spent on the poor. But this was a most costly sacrifice of love expressed by Mary, as she lavished Jesus with the perfume. Commentators say that as he hung on the cross, beaten battered and scourged beyond recognition; the fragrance of her sacrifice would have still been on Him and would have floated up to Him as he struggled to breathe, and been an encouragement to Jesus. It would have been a reminder to Him of His love for us and ours for Him as demonstrated by Mary.

Many in the church have become so busy with serving, programs and ministries and have neglected the One that they are serving. Loving Jesus and spending time with Him is the ultimate act of service. I can not even call it service as it is born of such gratitude for His love for us. Loving someone is a relationship. You don't get married and say to your spouse, "I love you" once and that's it. No, you keep the fire of your love burning as you spend time together. You do things that please each other and you are comfortable in each other's company, even when there are no words spoken. You get to know each other so well that you know what the other would say, and what they would do in situations. You learn to forgive each other and want the best for the other person. You become alike as you understand one another so well. That is the ideal scenario anyway! We can have that with Jesus if we pursue an intimate relationship with Him. He, of course, is perfect and is so gracious as He sees us as perfect too: never looking at our flaws. From that place of acceptance, He woos us with His love and transforms us into His likeness as He prepares us as His bride.

All you have to do is say yes. Song of Solomon, described as the most beautiful love song of all, opens with "let him kiss me." In the story, the young Shulamite woman, who is in love with him, thinks she is unworthy. She thinks she's too dark and has nothing to say or to offer. Mid- book, even though he has been expressing his love for her, she doesn't answer his knock, but then she realises how much she longs for him and pursues him again until she finds him.

We too pull back from the one who loves us and from an intimate relationship with Him when we are ashamed and don't feel worthy. It is only with Jesus that we can be healed and become whole, and He says we'll do this together. We are totally acceptable and loved by Him. Song of Songs 2:15 talks of the little foxes that spoil the vine. These are the little things that get in the way of our intimacy with the Lord. Thankfully, He says we will work it out together and in His presence there's no need to hide or be ashamed. He knows and understands all of our struggles. It brings healing and wholeness just being with Him. This is so beautiful and astounding. I used to sit for hours doing nothing, just opening My Heart in faith to Him and I would feel such peace and waves of His presence pouring over me: filling my heart, releasing my head, washing away all my striving, and my unworthiness. I would emerge from those times changed because you can't fail to be changed in His presence. He is everything.

Many of us, if not all, must encounter the Spirit of truth and love first as we begin to receive His love, tender affection, and unrelenting presence even in the midst of our biggest challenges. Here is where we find the compassion and the clarity to see who He has made us to be, and we get the opportunity to see Him. It is the truth of identity and in "Song of Songs," we witness the journey of the Shulamite coming fully alive.

It takes time, and the Shulamite has to repeatedly hear how Solomon loves her. He spoke his love over her again and again. He told her how one glance from her worshipping eyes stole his heart, and how he was held hostage by her love. He loved her into the fullness of her identity, until she was willing to grab hold of him and agreed to be his bride. Song of Songs 4:2 TPT reads, "When I look at you, I see how you have taken my fruit and tasted my word. Your life has become clean and pure, like a lamb washed and newly shorn.

You now show grace and balance with truth on display". Jesus is continually speaking this kind of love and identity over us just as Solomon did to the Shulamite, until she finally stops him in verse 6 and says "I have made up my mind." Until then she was going back and forth with Jesus, wrestling with shame and why she wasn't worthy, but at this point she relented and said, "Until the darkness disappears and the dawn has fully come, in spite of shadows and fears, I will go to the mountaintop with you– the mountain of suffering love and the hill of burning incense. Yes, I will be your bride." She bends under the weight of his love and as she yields to him is transformed from the Shulamite to the bride. She answers his longing knock. She opens the door and the revelation of his love continues to restore her. She comes alive.

As we too continue to lean into His love and let Him take us to the places in us that long for His love and redemption, the more His love will catch fire within us until all that remains is truth. This is the picture of continual love and revelation that then births our identity as the bride.

Here is where she and we rise in full identity as the bride:

"But now I have grown and become a bride, and my love for him has made me a tower of passion and contentment for my beloved. I am now a firm wall of protection for others, guarding them from harm. This is how he sees me–I am the one who brings him bliss, finding favour in his eyes." (Song of Songs 8:8-10 TPT)

This is our story too, as we allow His love to continue to woo us and transform us. I encourage you to spend time with Him and let Him into every area of your heart, allowing Him to change you. It won't always be easy but perseverance produces reward.

Song of Songs begins with the Shulamite saying of Solomon, "Let him kiss me with the kisses of his mouth," and "For your love is better than wine." So I want to ask, will you let Jesus do the same to you? You are called to be His Bride and one day soon, He is coming back to claim his betrothed and take them to the wedding feast which has been prepared in Heaven. Meanwhile, He wants to woo you and help you make yourself ready. He wants you to look at him unashamed. With one look of your eyes, He is undone. He is so in love with you and can't take His gaze away from you. He delights in you and everything about you is perfect to Him.

A lot of my journey has been discovering this. It may have taken decades, but God never gives up on us, for love conquers all.

"Arise, my love, my beautiful companion, and run with me to the higher place. For now is the time to arise and come away with me. (Song of Songs 2:13 TPT)

Chapter 17
BE-LIEVE IN YOUR FUTURE

"'For I know the plans I have for you,' declares the LORD, '
plans to prosper you and not to harm you,
plans to give you hope and a future'"
(Jeremiah 29:11 NIV).

Regardless of your current situation, God has great plans for you which He wants you to come into alignment with and this can take time. When we are born again, we still have our old ways of thinking. We need to have our minds renewed and our hearts healed, which is an ongoing process. It is called, "working out our salvation." As we keep our eyes fixed on Jesus and put our faith and hope in Him, believing His promises towards us, even when our circumstances tell us otherwise, we discover His faithfulness to His promises. Even when we do not see them fulfilled, we learn to trust Him. I love the scripture of 2 Timothy 2:13 from the Living Bible Translation, "Even when we are too weak to have any faith left, he remains faithful to us and will help us, for he cannot disown us who are part of himself, and he will always carry out his promises to us."

The greatest opposition to becoming the person God has called us to be often comes from those closest to us who do not understand or even like the changes they see in us. Not because they don't want the best for us, but change is always uncomfortable and can feel threatening. It is our families and loved ones who have known us the longest who often find it the hardest to embrace any changes and transformations in us as we get renewed in our thinking and become who we are truly called to be. I recall standing at the kitchen sink discussing with the children the meaning of the word vocation. My youngest one turned to me and asked, 'Mummy is your vocation to do the washing up?' That is how he saw me. To him I was a mummy who washed the dishes, prepared meals, did the housework and school runs, and indeed that was the season I was in. It did not define who I was and it certainly did not mean that I could not change as the children grew up and left home.

God reminded me of this event recently as I was reflecting on my past and I asked Him, "Lord, what is the truth about who I am as washer-up and mother?" Jesus said to me, "you are a mother and you will always be a mother," and He impressed upon me that the washing up was just one of the functions in that season of my life. It didn't define who I was. Nowadays, despite being nearly aged sixty, God has been telling me He has great plans for my life and for once I am beginning to embrace them and believe the truth of who I am in Him. With Him nothing is impossible. He has great plans for you too, no matter your age.

God will remind me at times of a vision I experienced in a crypt in Glastonbury, England some years ago. I'd descended a short flight of stone steps into the ancient crypt below Glastonbury Abbey during a women's prayer conference. I was in search of some solitude, hoping to spend some time alone with God. It was cold and bare in the crypt but someone had thoughtfully placed sheepskin rugs on the stone bench which ran along the walls of the little room. I decided to lie on one of the rugs and as I did so I had the impression that I was lying by a log fire, resting, comfortably warm, dozing without a care. I had a vision of Jesus and Father on the other side of the room, eyes locked and talking intently. I knew they were discussing me and the plans they had for me. Outside the old heavy wooden door stood two angels with swords crossed, protecting me and preventing anyone from entering. I have often been reminded of the vision and it's always comforting to know that God the Father and Jesus the Son are taking care of my life. The sheepskin rug represents the Holy Spirit, my comforter and guide on whom I lean and rest.

Recently, God brought me back to the same vision in which Father God came over to me and stroked my head with such tenderness, like a mother. Jesus, the express image of the father, also said that He was like a mother-hen watching over her chicks, in reference to His love for Jerusalem.

With the help of the Holy Spirit, He will complete the good work He has begun in you.

For I am confident of this very thing, that He who began a good work among you will complete it by the day of Christ Jesus. (Philippians 1:6, NASB)

Then said the Lord to me, You have seen well, for I am alert and active, watching over My word to perform it. (Jeremiah 1:12, AMP)

If you are struggling to trust God, you can pray like the father in chapter 9 of Mark's Gospel (NIV), whose son was possessed by a demon and having convulsions. The boy was brought to Jesus, "If you can do anything, take pity on us and help us" cried the father (v.22). Jesus assured the man that "everything is possible for one who believes" (v.23). "Immediately, the boy's father exclaimed, 'I do believe; help me overcome my unbelief!'" (v.24). Upon hearing the man's request, "I believe; help my unbelief!" Jesus immediately spoke to the unclean spirit and permanently cast it out of the boy.

Chapter 18
BE STRONG AND COURAGEOUS

"To the glistening eastern sea, I give you Queen Lucy the Valiant"

Spoken by Aslan in The Lion, the Witch and the Wardrobe by C.S. Lewis

One of my favourite books and films since childhood has been *The Lion, the Witch and the Wardrobe*, by C.S. Lewis. My favourite character is Lucy Pevensie, the youngest of 4 siblings sent to live in the English countryside with the eccentric Professor Kirke during World War II. Lucy discovers a wardrobe which she steps into and finds herself in the magical world of Narnia. When Lucy first tells her siblings of her visit to Narnia, they tease her mercilessly until they too stumble through the wardrobe into the magical land, where the ice queen reigns. I don't want to spoil the story too much in case you haven't had the joy of reading or watching it, but they eventually meet Aslan the lion who is the true King of Narnia. The children become heroes and later kings and queens. Of them all, Lucy is the most sensitive and faithful. She has a close and intimate relationship with Aslan, riding on his back and clinging to his mane as he goes into battle. She is courageous, strong and refuses to deny to her siblings that she went to Narnia. Eventually, they follow her through the wardrobe. Although she is gifted a dagger, she does not have to use it in battle. Lucy is a picture of how you can be: with childlike faith, trusting, courageous, never giving up, and clinging to the mane of the Lion. He fights your battles and will take you to victory.

Another film I love is the epic romance, *Titanic* (1997), in which a seventeen-year-old Rose sets sail from Southampton for New York with her wealthy fiancé and widowed mother to enter into a loveless marriage to a wealthy American called Hal. The purpose was to help save the family from falling from society into poverty. In a moment of despair, as she attempts to take her life by jumping from the stern railing, she is rescued by a poor young artist called Jack, played by Leonardo de Caprio whose first name means lion-hearted. They fall in love to the horror of her mother and anger of her fiancé who tries to fit Jack up by planting a valuable necklace on his person.

The ensuing drama of events and the tragedy of the sinking ship save Rose, but not Jack who perishes in the freezing waters as he tries to help Rose to safety. Despite this tragic turn of events, Rose was indeed very courageous as she promised Jack she would make the most of life before he disappeared into the ocean.

She is able to hide herself from Hal who is also one of the few survivors and go on to live a full life under a new name which she takes from Jack. True love rescued and empowered her to go on. Both Rose and Lucy showed great courage in the face of fierce opposition.

Courage can mean the ability to do something that is frightening or overwhelming or having strength to face ordeals.

I know all about fear: fear of the future, fear of failing, fear of success, fear of man, fear of doing something for the first time, fear of speaking in a group of people and so on. It can be crippling. Many of us discovered what real fear felt like for the first time with the onset of Covid in 2020. We listened to all the scaremongering, real or not, and we became fearful for our lives, for our children, and for the future.

Yet, I look back over my life and can see the times I have overcome fear. You should do the same. You will be amazed at what you have achieved that you may never have thought possible.

Looking back at my own experience, I am so grateful for the freedom I had as a child to experience the new and unknown and for the long reign my father gave me when it came to travel and trying new exploits. Then with Gordon, later in life, who has always jumped straight into what I would call massive challenges. Such as, deciding to bike ride 1000 miles from John O'Groats in Scotland to Lands End in the far south west corner of England, in order to raise money for charity, despite not having ridden a bike for decades. Another time we bought a sailing boat together and sailed all the way down to the isles of Scilly. I had never sailed prior to that yet I found myself clinging to the bow, harnessed in because of the swell and stormy seas, rigging in the sails. There are also memories of ski trips as a novice skier where Gordon would lead me down steep, icy, mogul covered runs. I was always pushing myself in response to his challenges to do more than I thought possible. I was often fearful and sometimes refused to go on, but filled with gratitude and a sense of achievement for those times that I didn't give up.

God understands how challenges that may not seem very big to others can overwhelm us. At those times, He may throw us into the deep end or take us gently step by step, always with us.

Whatever size your steps, I would say, just keep moving forward. I look back on my life and think of how I have persevered. I have approached boulders which transformed into stepping stones as I took them on and the fear shrank a little bit with each step.

There were times when I impetuously jumped straight in, knowing that if I didn't take immediate action then I never would. This culminated in rash decision making with unhappy consequences. At other times fear has prevented me from taking action and has led to disappointment and regret, usually with myself.

I always think of my youngest child as a little boy, worrying about his future: how he was going to manage at senior school or get into university, what career he should pursue, as he observed his older siblings doing all of those things. So often, we look ahead and wonder how we will ever succeed.

As a mother, I was able to allay his fears and tell him that by the time he was their age, he would not only be ready and equipped, but he would be excited as he anticipated the next stage of his life.

Another of my favourite books is *Hinds Feet on High Places*, by Hannah Hurnard, an allegory about a young woman called "Much Afraid." Based on Hannah's own fears, it is the story of Much Afraid's journey away from her Fearing family into the high places under the guidance of the Shepherd. In her sequel *Mountain of Spices*, Hannah says that the only way to grow and change is to overcome each fear as you face it.

"The very characteristics and weaknesses of temperament with which we were born, which often seem to us to be the greatest of all hindrances to the Christian life, are, in reality, the very things which, when surrendered to the Saviour, can be transformed into their exact opposites and can therefore produce in us the loveliest of all qualities".

"One must either succumb to the fearing nature altogether and become a "Craven Coward," for the rest of one's life; or by yielding that fearful nature wholly to the Lord and using each temptation to fear as opportunity for practising faith, be made at last into a radiant "Fearless Witness" to His love and power. There is no middle course." (Hannah Hurnard)

As you become freer in your identity, you will begin to start stepping into the plans and purposes that God has for you and that may mean you're going to have to start doing things that you've not done before or changing old habits. This will involve overcoming your fears: fear of failure, fear of success, fear of giving up, fear of doing it wrong, fear of what other people think. Remember, the bible tells us that perfect love casts out all fear. So, the most impactful revelation you can have is that God loves you.

When we hear God telling us to do something, often we will try to procrastinate and justify our objections by finding a scripture that validates our inaction or we seek someone who will agree with us and support our decision. We convince ourselves that we haven't heard from God.

We have to take those leaps of faith. Joyce Meyer, prolific Christian author and teacher, encourages us to face the fear and do it anyway. So many times, I know I have heard God's instruction and have had to block out the negative voices in my head or the advice from well-meaning people. It is often only *after* we have stepped out that God confirms it was right and then the peace comes.

Sometimes it's not a question of being courageous enough to take one giant step but learning daily to take small steps which aren't so daunting. As you move towards your goal, celebrate your achievement, however small.

Don't be hard on yourself when panic and fear overwhelm you again. Just go back into that place of peace with God. Remember, if He has told you to do it he will be with you and so it's a question of returning to a place of rest, not trying to do it again in your own strength, but just allowing Him to steer you and help you find that place of peace.

Who, then, are those who fear the Lord?
He will instruct them in the ways they should choose.
They will spend their days in prosperity,
and their descendants will inherit the land.
(Psalm 25:12-13, NIV)

You'll be amazed at how He opens up opportunities for you to take your next step.

Believing God is with you isn't always as easy as it sounds. The realisation that you aren't alone, and that God is with you takes time. Every time He shows up, you can put your trust in Him that little bit more. He shows up every time!

Difficulty in trusting Him is often rooted in our childhood. Children are so trusting and expect support, protection, and love from grown-ups, yet somewhere along the line, intentionally or unintentionally, they fail us and leave us feeling abandoned and rejected. The only person we learn to trust is ourselves. God wants us to know that He is Emmanuel, that He is always with us and that He was with us when we were going through those experiences where we felt alone, unprotected, and unguided. He is with us when we step out in faith and "face the fear anyway."

It always comes back to love because the love of God casts out all fear and there is no fear in love (1 John 4:18). A way to seek Him and get into the place of receiving God's love is through worship. It is the place where love is perfected and peace of mind is restored. By worshipping God, we are expressing our adoration and trust and as we lift Him up we begin to see from His perspective and learn His ways.

As the psalmist proclaims, "I sought the Lord, and He answered me, and delivered me from all my fears" (Psalms 34:4, ESV)

PART 4:

BUILDING A LIFE IN GOD

Chapter 19
MOVING FORWARD IN YOUR PURPOSE

According to the Oxford English Dictionary:

Purpose: "The reason for which something is done or created or for which something exists.

Synonyms: Design, aim, objective, goal
Connotation: Intention or what one intends to accomplish or attain

As we have discussed in previous chapters, we are made by God in His image, and that we need to know who we are, whose we are, how the Kingdom realm we come from functions and what our role is in it. In order for us to operate in our purpose, we have to reclaim our identity. Identity creates purpose.

We can have purpose but not identity and as I shared from my own experience, most of what I accomplished did not satisfy or bring fulfilment until I began to discover who I was and came into line with what God was calling me to do. He has gone before us and prepared the way and He has made us uniquely able to carry out the unique calling He has placed on each of our lives.

"For we are God's handiwork, created in Christ Jesus to do good works, which God prepared in advance for us to do" (Ephesians 2:10NIV).

God's Timing in Your Purpose

So often we have to wait for God's timing. He is never in the same hurry as us. I was always looking to the next thing, the next place, the next holiday hoping to find happiness in those experiences. Yet the satisfaction was always short lived as true happiness comes from inner joy which in turn comes from being totally secure in our identity. It comes from within us, not from what is happening around us. Happiness and happenings have the same root word referring to what is going on and what is occurring. True contentment doesn't not come because of our circumstances. Joy is a state found deep within and if you look at the lives of Joseph, David, Moses, and Jesus, they all had to learn this and to wait.

Being on the move in a nomadic lifestyle is quite common for those who are always in search of fulfilment. You have heard, no doubt, the phrase that the grass is greener on the other side, but clearly it isn't or we wouldn't keep moving on, be it geographically, in careers, relationships, etc. I can personally say "been there, done that, and got the T-shirt." It didn't bring satisfaction but longing.

There are seasons when God has to box us in to show us, we have been looking in the wrong places. Moses spent many years growing up in Egypt and then out in the fields as a shepherd before he was called to deliver his people. Joseph spent his childhood and early adult years in captivity and under Egyptian rule. David spent his early years in the sheepfold and later on the run even though he had been anointed King by the prophet, but it wasn't yet his time. Jesus was a carpenter's son and did not begin His ministry until He was thirty years old.

During such seasons, we are being refined and moulded with our hearts being healed. God knows exactly what He is doing with us. If we go ahead of His timing, it can cause us problems. Look at Moses, he killed the Hebrew man once he had discovered that he was a Hebrew. He wanted to help his people but he wasn't ready and acted impetuously and with anger. Then there was Joseph who bragged to his brothers about his dreams and who later asked Pharaoh's baker and cupbearer to put in a good word for him so that he could get out of prison. Again, it wasn't his time. David had to go and hide in caves and he nearly killed King Saul who he knew he was called to replace, but thankfully he held back and didn't commit the crime. I wonder what would have happened to his life and the nation of Israel had he been impetuous and killed Saul when he had the chance?

Only Jesus moved in God's perfect timing. He trusted in Him and rested in Him, waiting for His instruction. God sometimes boxes us in. He puts us in what seems like an endless season of inactivity. For some it is through an illness, or it could be being a stay-at-home mum. He knows what is best for us and it is in these times we learn to stand on His promises, even though we can't see any fruit. Like the story of the man who God told to push against a huge rock with all his might, which he did for many years; toiling in the mid-day sun, day in and day night but becoming frustrated and discouraged as the rock never budged, not even an inch. He began to feel he was a failure and that he was never going to succeed in the mission that God had set for him. He finally cried out to the Lord, asking Him why he was failing in the task. The Lord compassionately showed him how he had strengthened his muscles, built his faith, and obediently fulfilled the Lord's request.

Much of what God is doing with us in these seasons is not visible to the naked eye, and often everything we know is stripped away; all that we put our security in. It seems to us and to others that we are doing nothing with our lives. Don't despise these times. God is doing a deep work.

For me, He was rooting out fear, grounding me in love, removing wrong building blocks so I could get back to the foundations and then ensuring my foundations were correct. Without the right foundations the house will not stand. He hems us in and strips everything away and does heart healing, which can be painful. He wants to enlarge our capacity and to shore us up so we will succeed in all he has for us to do. First, He has to heal our hearts and rewire our thinking.

A Key to Fulfilling Your Purpose:

If you are like me and often end up on a treadmill of performance or perfectionism to do the task well or achieve your goals, as godly and directed by the Holy Spirit as they may be, you can become too focused on the job to the detriment of everything and everyone around you. While this can be commendable and an asset as you are seen as tenacious, efficient, and reliable to finish what you start; it can lead to a lot of stress and anxiety or fear of missing out when things don't go to plan, especially when curveballs are thrown at you which take you off course or give you delays. I know this very well!

Sometimes, it is true that the enemy is trying to thwart God's plans for you and prevent you from moving forward in your calling and destiny. However, it can be the old sinful nature of needing to perform to be accepted that is rearing its ugly head. The Lord will not leave us in our sinful nature and uses it to let us get to the end of ourselves so that we have to learn to lean completely on Him.

In such times, this calls for a deep surrender to the Lord. A letting go of trying to do things in one's own strength, and a trust in Him that He works all things for good. It may seem to you that you are diverging from the path, but God will bring you to the place you need to be. It is an unseen way, a hidden way, as on the surface, according to worldly ways, it looks like you are not getting anywhere but it is a surrender to Christ, a "letting go and letting God" This pleases God, and the more you are able to surrender your ways to Him, the easier you will find it when trials and obstacles arise, to let go and know He has it in hand. To know that He is faithful and that He will finish what He has begun. The end result will be so much more amazing than you could have dreamed or imagined, and you will give all the glory to God.

The choice is yours; to push yourself into exhaustion and allow anxiety, self-loathing, and condemnation for your failings to take over, or to let go and let God.

> ***Enlarge the place of your tent, And let them stretch out the curtains of your dwellings; Do not spare; Lengthen your cords, And strengthen your stakes. For you shall expand to the right and to the left, And your descendants will inherit the nations, And make the desolate cities inhabited. (Isaiah 54; 2-5 NKJV)***

Purpose Played Out In My Life

It's January 2015 and I find myself stepping off a plane onto the aeroplane stairs at Entebbe airport, Uganda. Memories of a short-lived return to Nigeria forty-five years previously come flooding back: the wall of heat that took my breath away, and the shimmering haze as the sun blistered the tarmac. Then, I was with my father and little sister trying to rebuild our shattered lives. Now, on African soil again for the first time in nearly half a century, I am coming to help rebuild the lives of others. Of course, I don't know that as I step into the bright light of an African summer's day and scan the horizon beyond the trees bordering the mass of concrete on the runway. If I had known on that January day all that God had in store for me and my family, I doubt I would have felt so intrepid.

All I know is that it feels like coming home. Excitement and anticipation begin to stir up as the call for adventure and the unknown beckons and because I'm excited to be going with my friend Clare and a handful of other new acquaintances to a Christian conference in Kampala hosted by Dr. John Mulinde, founder of international ministry, World Trumpet Mission. I tentatively allow myself to feel sensations I haven't experienced since I was young; it's like dipping my toe into the normally bracing Atlantic Ocean and discovering it's deliciously warm and inviting.

How have I ended up here? I ponder how five years previously our children's senior school invited families to host members of an Ugandan children's choir who were on a three month tour of England to raise money for their orphanage. The group comprised teachers, pastoral leaders and children aged eleven to nineteen. We offered to house two and ended up taking in the headmaster and a young man named Robert; a nineteen-year-old orphan who was the drummer in the choir.

It wasn't a prayerful decision but an idea I almost discarded, yet one that would have huge ramifications as we later discovered how we were fitting into God's plan for our lives which would knit together hearts from two continents. It would bring hope and a realisation of not being forgotten to a small rural Ugandan community as well as meaning, purpose and a capacity to love others, which we didn't know we had, to our family in the southwest corner of England.

Meeting Robert changed our lives: first we gained a son, and eventually a community. After his whirlwind tour of the United Kingdom, he returned to his home, a small mud-brick house that he lived in with an old lady he called "grandma," who had taken him in, and subsequently three other children after losing their parents. Some of "grandma's" biological children were buried in the garden under mounds of grass-covered soil that looked like ant hills, the only reminder of their tragically shortened lives.

We continued to help and financially support him through his education and by contributing to small projects in his home: a water tank, pigs, a new roof.

When I had the opportunity to go to the conference in Kampala, I knew that I couldn't miss the chance to visit Robert in his village near Lake Victoria.

So here I was on the top step of the plane about to begin an adventure that continues to this day. At the end of the conference, Robert picked me up and took me on a three-hour drive to Masaka, a town in South West Uganda on the edge of Lake Victoria, crossing the equator on route, until we arrived at a seedy but, according to Robert, "safe" hotel. *Safe from what?,* I wondered! He settled me in for the night before disappearing in a cloud of dust after promising to return at 9 am the following morning to take me to his church; a tiny mud-brick building in a clearing in a mango grove. That was the first I'd heard of his connection with God. I would soon discover he was a believer and youth pastor of Kyantale Victory Church. I would also discover that Ugandans do not have the same concept of time as we do in the West. This would become a recurring theme.

So, having waited an hour for Robert's arrival, he finally turned up in the same taxi, covered by now in a thick layer of dust from navigating the nontarmacked dirt roads of the African bush. He bundled me into the back seat, informed me we were going to his church, a 30-minute drive away, and that not only was I the guest of honour but also the guest speaker. I had to think fast about what I would share while simultaneously trying to hold a conversation with Robert as we bounced over potholes, scraped past overgrown bushes, and tried to avoid the tide of humanity out on the roads, notwithstanding the odd cow or goat.

God was propelling me into my destiny and not giving me the chance to squirm out of it.

So began a series of events engineered and implemented by God, as I and my family learned to partner with Him and the community as we raised money to build a church, buy land to grow coffee and pineapples, set up a chicken farm, build two water tanks for the village, co-labour with another ministry to run medical missions, and so much more.

Some of the fundraising took us out of our comfort zone and stretched us immensely as Gordon, for example, announced one day that he was going to cycle solo from John O'groats in Scotland to Lands End in Cornwall, a distance of nearly a thousand miles over ten days, to raise awareness and much needed funds. If that wasn't challenging enough, he didn't even own a bike nor had he ridden one for years.

Taking up the challenge changed our lives in so many unexpected ways as we both regularly cycle together now as a hobby and take cycling holidays to stunning destinations where the efforts of strenuous climbing are rewarded with stunning views, a huge sense of achievement and the joy of doing this together. Our involvement with Robert has personally led me into numerous impromptu undertakings, such as preaching at a church service or sharing my personal testimony with a crowd of over a hundred people who had walked on foot for miles to be seen at the medical mission and were now patiently waiting their turn to be seen. Watching the grandmothers cry as I shared about the loss of my mother and then putting their hands up to receive Jesus was so humbling as I knew their stories were far more harrowing than mine and also that God had used me this way. There is a generation of orphans in Uganda as a consequence of war and aids and so most are personally acquainted with death. I have prayed for the sick and received sacrificial gifts in gratitude that have touched me deeply, such as a few eggs, a pineapple, a bunch of bananas.

I have visited Robert five times now, including flying out at short notice when he was having a personal crisis in his life. We face constant challenges, have made numerous mistakes and sometimes I have done very little and feel immense guilt, only to remember that this is and always has been God's enterprise and I am just invited to do my part. At other times I feel like giving up, but at the end of the day I know we are in God's will, that He has given me and my family a sense of purpose, and more than that, another son and a community we love. How can you give up on someone who has become your son? How can you abandon a community who have nothing, keep you in their prayers and are so grateful that they haven't been forgotten.

God has plans and purposes for our lives that are far greater than anything we could ever imagine. They challenge, stretch and transform us completely as our hearts are expanded and entwined with others. As we partner with the limitless God of the universe, we are speechless and in awe of who He is and what He can do through and in us that will change us forever as our hearts are pierced with His love. We find ourselves far beyond our comfort zones and limited capabilities. I have discovered that His love binds us together like glue and moves us forward into our destinies.

Leaning into God

So often we try to do things on our own or go ahead of God, as we have seen in the biblical examples above. We become exhausted and inevitably our plans start to go wrong. God wants us to trust Him with all our heart and to put all our confidence in Him. I have learned this many times in our exploits in Uganda.

Most of us know Proverbs 3:5-6 NIV, "Trust in the LORD with all your heart and lean not on your own understanding; in all your ways submit to him, and he will make your paths straight."

But do we actually do that?

"You desire but do not have, so you kill. You covet but you cannot get what you want, so you quarrel and fight. You do not have because you do not ask God" (James 4:2 NIV)

The world will tell us to fight if that's what it takes. Driven by envy for what they want, James' readers are frustrated when they keep coming up empty. So they fight. James identifies their root problem; these believers in God refused to trust Him to provide what they needed.

I noticed as well that I am very good at asking God on behalf of others but neglect my own needs or doubt that what God does for others he will do for me.

The more time you spend with Him and discover how passionate He is for you and longing to give you His love, to protect you and to provide for you, the easier you will find it to run to Him whenever life throws a curveball at you. When your world is disrupted and you don't know what to do, when someone hurts you, when you have important decisions to make about your future, and basically everything else, you will run to Him! Take all your worries, cares, and needs to Jesus.

Keep on asking, and you will receive what you ask for. Keep on seeking, and you will find. Keep on knocking, and the door will be opened to you. (Matt. 7:7 NLT)

Walking with Wisdom

Proverbs 9:10 tells us that wisdom begins with fear of God. Not the kind of fear that makes you scared of punishment but one that comes from awe and reverence. The book of Proverbs gives us wisdom from above.

> *"We cross the threshold of true knowledge when we live in obedient devotion to God, Stubborn know-it-alls will never stop to do this, for they scorn true wisdom and knowledge"*
> *(Proverbs 7:1-9 TPT)*

Pay close attention, my child, to your father's wise words and never forget your mother's instructions. For their insight will bring you success, adorning you with grace-filled thoughts and giving you reins to guide your decisions. When peer pressure compels you to go with the crowd and sinners invite you to join in, you must simply say, "no."

Wisdom is our helper. The Holy Spirit living inside of us is the spirit of wisdom and wise counsel. The Bible is our instruction manual for right living. God has made His wisdom available to us so we can make right decisions and we have the mind of Christ. We have to actively pursue wisdom, to seek it as though searching for hidden treasure and to be teachable. It is a gift from a generous God. It sets us free as it is so full of grace.

Let me give you a simple example; when someone speaks a hurtful or accusing word the world will tell us to retaliate. Our natural and soulish inclination will be to rise up in indignation. We may retort with harshness ourselves as we become offended. We have chosen to allow that word to hurt us and define us. Wisdom tells us to turn the other cheek, to forgive that person, to pour oil on the situation by coming in the opposite spirit, and to be humble to see if what that person said actually has truth in it. Wisdom also gives the grace to do all of that and wisdom will become our shield of protection as we come into the fear of the Lord and do it His way.

"My child, will you treasure my wisdom? Then, and only then, will you acquire it. And only if you accept my advice and hide it within will you succeed. So train your heart to listen when I speak and open your spirit wide to expand your discernment – then pass it on to your sons and daughters. Yes, cry out for comprehension and intercede for insight. For if you keep seeking it like a man would seek for sterling silver, searching in hidden places for cherished treasure, then you will discover the fear of the Lord and find the true knowledge of God. Wisdom is a gift from a generous God, and every word he speaks is full of revelation and becomes a fountain of understanding within you. For the Lord has a hidden storehouse of wisdom made accessible to his godly ones. He becomes your personal bodyguard as you follow his ways, protecting and guarding you as you choose what is right" (Proverbs 2:1-9, TPT).

Wisdom will empower you to make the right decisions as you walk into your destiny and true pleasure will enter your soul if you follow good counsel. The understanding you gain will protect you from making poor choices and from those who don't speak truthfully and would take you off the path by their deception.

"For all my godly lovers will enjoy life to the fullest and will inherit their destinies." Proverbs 2:21 (TPT)

Chapter 20
REDEMPTION AND LOVE

Set me as a seal upon your heart, as a seal upon your arm;
for love is strong as death, passion fierce as the grave.
(Song Of Songs 8:6, TPT).

As we near the end of this book, that has taken us on a journey to discover identity, especially as the beloved, it seems appropriate to share a little bit about how love has been weaved throughout my life and my discovery that the redemptive power of God's love has always been at work.

As frail human beings who love inadequately, even though loved ones die, our love for them continues on. How much more the power of love which comes from God, who *IS* love, who sacrificed His one and only beloved son for you and me because He loves us so much.

The love of God transcends feeling and emotion and powerfully works on our behalf. He knows what is best for us. He fights for us, protects us and always wants our good even when we are in sin, rebellion, and don't know Him. He never gives up on us.

I have made a lot of messes in my life, but God is in the redemption and restoration business. His love for me meant that He was with me through those times, but that He also wants to give back everything that has been stolen, lost or damaged. In my pursuit of wisdom, in my pursuit of a relationship with Him and in my willingness to let Him heal my heart and change my wrong thinking, He has taken me on a journey (which I will be on into eternity) of getting healed and whole. The parts of my heart that I had built walls around to protect myself have been coming down and his transforming love has been healing me from the lies I had believed about myself and others. God is the way, the truth, and the life.

Proverbs 4:23 says we should protect our heart as our lives depend on what flows from it. When not nurtured or loved properly, and when hurt by others, children especially learn to protect their hearts by putting up walls around them. These are safeguards which God has allowed for our protection. We then see life through distorted lenses. For example, if we have been let down and abandoned enough times, we may choose not to ever get close to people again. That way, at least, we won't get hurt again. We may start to believe that people don't actually care about us and that we are dispensable.

God wants to bring truth to the lies that we have believed so that we can walk in freedom.

***"Behold, You desire truth in the inward parts,
And in the hidden part You will make me to know wisdom.
Purge me with hyssop, and I shall be clean;
Wash me, and I shall be whiter than snow. (Psalm 51:5 NKJV)***

In writing this book, God has taken me back to the beginning of my own life and helped me rewrite the narrative. He has shown me what I believed from my experiences and the walls of protection I put up around my heart. He has brought truth to my heart which has been setting me free and bringing down my protective walls.

God is outside of time. Think of your life as a carnival made up of lots of different floats which represent the different parts of your life. The procession begins. You are on the sidewalk watching the stream of floats and performers go by. You can only see one segment of your life at a time. But God is above observing everything. He knows where you have come from and where you're going and what makes up every part of your life.

Even when we didn't know God, He was with us because He is Emmanuel which literally means *God with us* and He, who never breaks a promise and who thought us up and spoke us into being says, He will never leave us or abandon us.

We can't change past events, but it is possible to rewire our mind and heart. We allow God to look into our hearts, thereby changing how we react to our past which in turn will inform our identity.

"Search me, O God, and know my heart: Try me, and know my thoughts: And see if there be any wicked way in me, And lead me in the way everlasting." Psalm 139:23-24 (KJV)

Recently, Jesus revealed to me that I needed to be reconciled to my mother. I needed to forgive her and not judge her for her absence and inability to give me what I needed when I was young. I didn't know I felt that way towards her. I'd put up walls of self-reliance long before and had become numb of any emotion towards my mother– good or bad. I'd made her out in my imagination to be unattached and uninterested toward me, when in fact that was what I had become to protect myself from the pain of having lost her. In a way, I blamed her for leaving me. Jesus showed me that I needed to repent of judging her and forgive her for going away. He allowed me to see her as she is now in heaven: perfect, loving, kind, and reaching out to me with a mother's unconditional all-embracing love. That was so healing and has altered how I see my past and helped me to move forward. I am seeing the whole procession!

As a child I used to have to tidy up the family bookcase. Dad persuaded me to do it by telling me I was the best in the family at the task. Always looking for affirmation I lapped that up and took on the job with great gusto thinking I was better than all my siblings and that's why my father chose me to do it!

Jesus took me back to that time. I was seven years old, sitting on the floor, lining up the books in order of size along the low white shelf in the sitting room. In the picture I saw Mummy, sitting close by, watching me with Jesus,

His hand gently brushing her shoulder, standing behind the back of the chair, both tenderly watching me. Of course, you may be asking, how could she be there as she'd been dead a couple of years. I believe the Lord showed me this to help me break free of some lies and pain. In this vision, I felt Mummy's pleasure, not just because I was her beloved daughter but because she too loved books and liked order and would herself have found pleasure as a child in tidying the bookcase. That gave me a sense of joy; that there was something that actually bonded us. I'd always thought people said we were alike because of our looks but God was showing that we had similarities in character.

God allowed me to see their love and appreciation of each other. He was inviting me to be a part of that too. I was a little jealous to be honest, but Jesus was inviting me into the same relationship with Him. He told me that as I forgave my mother, that my own intimacy with Him would grow. Jesus prays the Father to forgive us our sins as we forgive others. We can be saved yet walk in unforgiveness. We will still go to heaven but the unforgiveness becomes a blockage to our relationship with God while we're still on earth.

The pain of our experiences when not dealt with in the right way can lead to bitterness, resentment, unforgiveness and offence. All of these build walls that separate us from God. A key to pulling down those walls is to forgive. Letting the other person off the hook and no longer blaming them for your situation doesn't mean that you're endorsing what happened to you, but it means that you are handing the responsibility over to God. You become responsible for yourself. So when others hurt you in the future, you don't have to receive it if you choose not to get offended or judge or blame them. If you walk in forgiveness and only believe what God says about you to be true, you will find freedom to be loved and to love. You will find rest for your soul.

Chapter 21
HOUSE ANALOGY

My Father's house has many rooms; if that were not so, would I have told you that I am going there to prepare a place for you? And if I go and prepare a place for you, I will come back and take you to be with me that you also may be where I am. (John 14 :2 NIV)

I used to live in a grade 2 listed three-story house built in the 1780's in the county of Kent, aka The Garden of England. Once the stables in the grounds of a manor house and tucked at the bottom of a long drive lined with ancient poplars and plane trees, it was later converted to garages for the owner's cars and following that a home which when we bought it was dilapidated and in much need of renovation. With the help of my father-in-law, a builder by trade, we proceeded to restore it. Although it didn't have a basement there was a damp outhouse which was accessible by a low door, steps from the kitchen, and an attic with wasps nests in the rafters from where a hidden mice-run wended its way in a cavity between the inner and outer walls down to the kitchen. We loved that house and put a lot of love, attention, and money into restoring it. We began raising our family there, bringing all three children from the local maternity hospital to this, their first home. So it was quite a wrench to leave it behind and move to Cornwall where we are now.

Our new coastal home couldn't have been in greater contrast, a *new build* with open plan living. No longer surrounded by green fields in summer which turned to muddy quagmires in winter due to the heavy clay soil. We now had the ocean on our doorstep. The expanse of sea and sky were overwhelming in their beauty, but we also had to contend with ferocious winds, salty, damp air, the summer influx of tourists, and the season becoming longer every year as our beautiful little corner of the world became increasingly popular.

Having moved house so often throughout my life you would have thought the transition would be easy for me, but unlike the rest of the family who adapted like fish to water, (literally), I missed our home in Kent which we'd invested so much in emotionally and financially, as well as friends, family and the proximity to London. Moreover, our new home, being open plan, meant that there was nowhere to escape to. Especially now that we also had a large dog with few boundaries and muddy paws, who enjoyed not only sleeping on the sofa but who, to this day, causes me to jump out of my skin whenever she leaps over the back of said sofa every time the doorbell rings.

I would have dreams of our old home, sometimes that there were rooms hidden below the ground floor or in the attic that I was too afraid to venture into. When I was a teenager, I worked at weekends in a hotel as a chambermaid. It was an old building which had a couple of bedrooms in the eaves. All the chambermaids hated going up there as someone once said they had seen a ghost. There certainly was an eeriness and I don't think the rooms ever got cleaned properly as we would do the job as fast as we could before making a hasty getaway.

Our memories can be like rooms we don't want to revisit as they bring up pain and trauma. Some rooms seem too painful to enter, others are forgotten like cobwebs in the corner of a dusty old attic. Not all the memories are bad. As I began to look back over my past to write this book, memories would float to the surface at the most unexpected times. I enjoyed reminiscing in those moments, savouring them as pleasurable morsels.

One of our family's favourite Christmas films is *National Lampoon's Christmas.* Clark Wilhelm Griswold wants to have a special "Griswold Family Christmas," and after months of careful planning, he invites both of his parents, his wife's parents, his uncle Louis, and his senile aunt Bethany to join his family. Clark even prepares his house for Christmas with over 20,000 lights and a tree.

A few days before Christmas he goes to hide some presents in the attic while the family all get ready to go on a pre-Christmas shopping spree, but he ends up locked in the attic for the day while the family thinks he's disappeared to work on getting the light display up and running. He passes the time by watching family reels of past Christmases, wrapped in his mother's old fur coat and hat, crying his eyes out as he watches film footage of his childhood.

It was only many years later that God began to show me that our lives are filled with rooms that we dare not enter or don't even know exist as we've locked the door and thrown away the key. Perhaps memories that are too painful to bring up, or perhaps we've shut off a relationship, and erected walls to stop people getting to know the real us. There are also good ones that He wants to restore to us. Perhaps, we only remember the difficult side of a relationship we had with our parents, but God wants to redress the balance and show us the truth.

In writing this book and allowing myself to be more vulnerable and real about who I am, the walls have been progressively coming down and I've learned to enjoy "open plan" living. The light pours in so much more easily than in our old house in Kent with its thick walls, many rooms and where you could actually spend the day avoiding each other if you wanted. God wants to shine his light into the dark hidden places in our lives. We believe lies that keep us locked in shame and self-loathing, but if we would allow him in (He knows it all anyway and nothing can shock him), we will find freedom. Adam and Eve hid and blamed each other rather than admit their sin. God's nature is love. Love is long suffering. Love forgives. Love restores. Don't let the enemy keep you locked up in guilt and shame.

God has had the last laugh, as not only have I become more transparent and open towards my own family and friends, but we have welcomed many people in the last couple of years to share our annex which we converted during covid into a paid guest suite. I've come a long way!

It was in that house in Kent, while I was quietly breast feeding my daughter in her bedroom, in the wee hours of a winter's morning before the sun came up over the fields at the back of our house, that I invited Jesus into my life to be my Lord and Saviour. It was such a simple prayer, asking him to come and live inside my heart. He quietly moved in that day, taking up residence, and bringing a peace I'd never known. The Son of Man has nowhere to lay his head but He knocked at my door that day and I said *yes.*

As I made Him my Lord, little did I know that He was going to start to take my man-made walls of protection down and take me back to the foundations so that He could rebuild my life on Him, the Rock of Truth and revelation.

When we receive Jesus into our lives, He comes and lives in our hearts. There is no doubt that we are now saved, we have been made new and we can have an ongoing daily relationship with Jesus. There are times when we don't always sense him and can doubt His presence. The thing is we come with a lot of baggage: wrong mindsets, hurts, unforgiveness and offences. These all block our intimacy with him. Yet He doesn't just want to visit occasionally or be a distant acquaintance but longs to dwell in us; so begins a work of restoration, healing, and a long term project which can take years.

Kevin Zadai, Founder of Warrior Notes, died and came back to life during a routine dental surgery and found himself face to face with Jesus.

Forty-five minutes with the Savior radically transformed his life and ministry. He describes our relationship with Jesus this way:

The first phase is the state of revelation, when the Holy Spirit comes in and reveals Jesus to you. The second phase is visitation when you have visits by the Holy Spirit in one form or another and it's a very edifying time but it doesn't always stay permanent. Then there's a phase we can move into which Jesus referred to in the book of John. He said, "If you love me, I and my father will come and live with you", and this is very important because if you read the word studies in the original languages, it shows that they will actually bring their furniture and move in. Isn't it wonderful to know that God wants to come and live with you?" (*Awakening*, Kevin L. Zadai).

"I want to inhabit people. I want habitation of the spirit of God, where people will not grieve the Holy Spirit. They will walk with me without hindrance."

This is the final phase that Jesus showed Kevin who said Jesus told him, "I want to inhabit people. I want habitation of the spirit of God, where people will not grieve the Holy Spirit. They will walk with me without hindrance." Zadai discovered that this was going to require some adjustments, and a letting go of things in order to experience Jesus' and Father's presence permanently without blockages.

Thankfully, we can ask God to help us. Jesus is the architect, the master builder and He always finishes well.

House Plan

"For we are God's fellow workers, you are God's field, you are God's building" (1 Corinthians 3:9NKJV).

Think of yourself as a house with foundations and an attic. God is standing at your front door, knocking, and waiting to be invited in if you will let Him as He desires to have a relationship with you. He is a gentleman and will never come in uninvited. If you invite Him into your heart, He wants to make His home with you, but there can be work to do to renovate the house and to open up rooms that may have been locked for a long time. We are a work in progress and although we are saved, we have to work out what our salvation means and this involves having our minds renewed with the truth of scripture. We have to declutter, getting rid of the old to make room for more of Jesus and His word.

"I want to inhabit people. I want habitation of the spirit of God, where people will not grieve the Holy Spirit. They will walk with me without hindrance." (Kevin Zadai)

Even when you have made Him your Lord and saviour, He will always honour your heart, just like you would hope family members would knock before entering the bathroom when you are in it! And if you have locked the door and have no-go areas in your heart He gently woos you until you are ready to open them up.

This should be your home where you are loved, cherished, nurtured and your identity established in a safe environment so that when you go out into the world you are secure in who you are and take Jesus with you.

Let's enter the house and wander through the rooms together.

The Front Door

Once you have welcomed Him through the front door, He comes to make His home with you. This means you can run to Him any time like a child coming home from school at the end of the school day, who barges through the door, throws down their bag and grabs a snack. You can jump into His lap and share what you have been up to, your plans and hopes, your needs and concerns.

Let us therefore come boldly to the throne of grace, that we may obtain mercy and find grace to help in time of need.
Hebrews 4:16 (NKJV)

And He wants to share with you too. Too often we do all the talking; asking for things He has already promised to give us in His word and while God is a good listener, He already knows all about us and what is best for us. He wants to share what is on His heart.

The Sitting Room

After we have discharged our list of needs to the Father, we often jump down in a hurry, rushing off to do whatever worldly thing is on our minds.

How He loves for us to linger and spend time with Him, in worship or even in silence. Like a married couple who are content, we need times of relaxation to recharge as well; just as God rested on the seventh day and commanded the Israelites to take a weekly sabbath rest. When we are totally at rest, we are effectively letting God know that we trust Him for our lives, and that He is handling every need and situation.

The Dining Room

We need physical sustenance daily or we will waste away. How much more do we need the nourishment God gives us from His rhema word, as we spend time meditating on it and feasting on His goodness? To meditate is to contemplate and to chew on like a cow chews the cud. It can also mean to mutter or speak aloud. Faith comes by hearing so as we speak out what the Bible says and receive the revelation that it brings to our hearts, our faith is built up.

The dining room can also represent times of fellowship with other believers, just as Jesus enjoyed meals with His disciples and followers. This could be sharing bread and wine together which brings us into communion and oneness with Him and each other.

There was often joy and feasting, like at the wedding in Cana, and He prepares a banqueting table for us, even in the presence of our enemies.

The Study

In the study, we spend time delving into the word of God. Many of us find this difficult and hard to do routinely. I know I do! I think I have read Genesis more times than any other book in the Bible as my good intentions to read the Bible in a year don't get further than that.

Honestly, I don't have the solution, other than suggesting taking bite size pieces and not beating yourself up by getting religious about it. Ask God to help you and ask the Holy Spirit to breathe on your daily reading. He is the helper, and He has the mind of Christ.

Look for Jesus in all you read. The Bible may seem like a boring history book, but it is *His Story*. Some even say that the Old Testament is irrelevant but as Augustine famously described: The new is the old revealed; the old is the new concealed. So they cannot be separated from each other. It has also been said that the Old Testament is the foundations and walls while the New is the roof. Without the foundations, the roof would collapse, and without the roof, the house would leak and fall down.

The Foundations

"Now, therefore, you are no longer strangers and foreigners, but fellow citizens with the saints and members of the household of God, having been built on the foundation of the apostles and prophets, Jesus Christ being the Chief Cornerstone, in whom the whole building, being fitted together, grows into a holy temple of the Lord, in whom you also are being built together for a dwelling place of God in the Spirit."
Ephesians 2:19-22 (NKJV)

Every house needs foundations and these can slow down construction, but are essential. Too many of us are in a hurry to get things done in our lives. If a house is built incorrectly the builder may have to go back to the foundations to rebuild it. That is what Jesus told me He was doing with me when He pulled me out of all the ministries and occupations in which I was involved. He also began stripping me of religious thinking and wrong mindsets. He had to "unteach" me from what I had learned, even in Christian settings.

Remember the story of *The Three Little Pigs*? One built his house of straw and one of sticks, which were built in no time. How they laughed at their brother when theirs were finished but his house was still only constructed as far as the foundations as he was building with bricks.

However, once his house was built, on a starlit night a wolf came by to eat up the three little pigs and he blew the straw house and the stick house down, but no matter how hard he huffed and puffed, he was unable to blow down the house made of bricks.

The third little pig took his brothers into the safety of his home, but he admonished them. "What did I tell you? he said. It's important to build houses properly!"

There was a house on the opposite side of the valley to our home. It sold recently to a couple from out of town. It looked okay to the naked eye, but it had no foundations and when the storms came, which they do fiercely here as we face the ocean, the whole house quaked, and the wind whistled through every nook and cranny. They have decided to completely demolish the house and start again at great cost to ensure the house will stand for decades to come.

In every stone building, one stone is crucial. It is laid first, and it is to ensure that the building is square and stable. It is the rock upon which the weight of the entire structure rests. It is the cornerstone. Scripture describes Jesus as the *Chief Cornerstone* of our faith. As the Chief Cornerstone, Jesus ensures the stability of the whole system of our salvation. Jesus was and is the only plan of salvation.

> ***Therefore this says the Lord God: 'Behold, I lay in Zion a stone for a foundation, a tried stone, a precious cornerstone, a sure foundation." Isaiah 28:16 (NKJV)***

Some Biblical scholars believe Jesus was a stonemason and not a carpenter which would make sense of the scriptures about him as the chief cornerstone. Our faith in Him is foundational.

> ***"Listen to me, you who pursue righteousness and who seek the Lord: Look to the rock from which you were cut and to the quarry from which you were hewn; look to Abraham, your father, and to Sarah, who gave you birth." (Isaiah 51:1 NIV)***

Abraham was the father of faith, the faith we have because of God's grace towards us. We can find strength in the fact that we have been hewn from a solid and stable rock, that is Jesus.

The Basement

Basements are a bit like attics, where things get chucked and forgotten, such as tools and equipment that we think we might need again one day. What is in your basement that you no longer need and could get rid of completely?

What if there is something that would be very useful to you now, but you didn't need in your last season? Maybe God wants to revive forgotten or abandoned dreams.

Are there any areas of your life that need fixing, but you have neglected? Areas that God may be wanting you to restore like relationships, wrong habits, or good habits that you have stopped doing?

The Bathroom

Once we are saved God accepts us as righteous and holy because of His son's perfect sacrifice on the cross in our place. However, our fallen nature means that we will continue to sin and make mistakes which can get in the way of our personal relationship with God. John 13:10-12 MSG, "Jesus said, 'If you've had a bath in the morning, you only need your feet washed now and you're clean from head to toe. My concern, you understand, is holiness, not hygiene. So now you're clean. But not every one of you'". He knew who was betraying Him. That's why he said, "Not every one of you." After He had finished washing their feet, He took His robe, put it back on, and went back to His place at the table.

We are clean because we are washed in his blood, but we must daily check our hearts, motives, and actions to ensure we are not blocking our relationship with Him. This takes care of hygiene. Daily we can ask the Holy Spirit to search our hearts and then repent of anything He shows us. It is important when we have repented sincerely to believe that God has forgiven us and not try and pick it up again or feel guilty and condemned. That is the enemy speaking. As we continue to keep short accounts in our walk with God, we will hear His voice more clearly and recognise His voice versus that of the accuser. We can wash, knowing He has washed us clean. We can look in the mirror like the psalmist in Psalm 34 and be unashamed.

The Bedroom

My favourite room apart from the fact that I love snuggling under the duvet on a cold winter's night!

This is a place for intimate connection with the Lord. It is for the battle weary who need to take off their armour, lay down their weapons and rest. It is for those who are so caught up in ministry or careers that they have neglected their first love. It is for exhausted mamas who need to lay down their heads and be refreshed and built up again, even for a short while as He understands how busy they are in this season. It is for those who long for a deeper, more intimate relationship with the Lord.

It is for all who desire to spend more quality time with Jesus, to get to know Him better, and to receive healing and revelation. It is the place of transformation.

If you want to ignite your personal time with God on a regular basis, I can recommend a book called *Secrets of the Secret Place* by Bob Sorge in which he says, "I have written this book with passion to empower and inspire your secret relationship with God." In it, he presents keys for developing your personal relationship with Jesus.

The Attic

I think of the attic being full of childhood memories, old photos, heirlooms, memories we have filed away as they were too painful to process, or good memories that we would do well to recollect as Clark Griswald did or when we, as children, watched our family slideshow to recall Mummy.

I don't often go rummaging through the attic. Likewise, don't always go looking to dig up the past, but allow God to bring up what he wants in His timing. Maybe there is healing needed or maybe it is to revive fond memories of someone or discover truth about a relationship which we had seen through a lens of our own brokenness.

The Walls

These refer to the walls which we build around our hearts to protect ourselves, especially as children.

God has put that system in place to protect our hearts as they are so valuable, are very vulnerable to attack and are the source wellspring of everything we do.

"Above all else, guard your heart, for everything you do flows from it." (Proverbs 4:23 NIV)

Having once protected us, there comes a time when God wants to pull the walls down. They have served their purpose in guarding our hearts and God understands and honours that but He gently woos us and invites us to let our guard down so he can come in and heal that part of us that we have been protecting. He desires our whole heart.

"Love the Lord your God with all your heart and with all your soul and with all your strength and with all your mind, and your neighbour as yourself." (Luke 10:27, NIV)

It can take time to bring those walls down and God will do it the best way He knows for us, if we give Him permission.

The Roof

In his first letter to the Corinthians, the apostle Paul writes that love should be the motivation of our lives. He begins chapter 13 in *The Passion Translation* by saying, "If I were to speak with eloquence in earth's many languages, and in the heavenly tongues of angels, yet I didn't express myself with love, my words would be reduced to the hollow sound of nothing more than a clanging cymbal." How often we act and speak, paying lip service but the motive of our hearts is not one of love. Moreover, we may think we are being loving because we're not acting or speaking maliciously, jealously, disrespectfully, or selfishly. Bill Johnson, senior leader of Bethel Church, Redding, California goes as far as to say that the opposite of love is indifference. Jesus ostracised the church of Laodicea in His letter to the churches in the Book of Revelation for becoming lukewarm, distracted and more interested in wealth. He said that because they were neither hot nor cold, he would spit them out of his mouth. He entreats them to open up the door of their hearts to let him in. He is standing there knocking, waiting to be invited in, wanting to give them a feast at his table.

True love, according to Paul, is a place of safety.

"Love bears all things, believes all things,
hopes all things, endures all things."
(1 Corinthians 13:7 EST)

The Passion translation describes love in verse 7 as "a safe place of shelter for it never stops believing the best for others. Love never takes failure for defeat, for it never gives up."

The author, Dr. Brian Simmons, explains that the verb "to bear" is actually the word for *roof* as in Mark 2:4 (NIV), "Since they could not get him to Jesus because of the crowd, they made an opening in the roof above Jesus by digging through it and then lowered the mat the man was lying on."

Dr. Simmons believes Paul is saying that love covers all things like a roof covers the house and that like a roof protects and shields, it provides a safe place that offers shelter, not exposure. (see Simmon's notes to 1 Cor.13:7). God wants us to be like that for others, sincerely and passionately loving them, not exposing their failures and weaknesses but also to honour ourselves. God will never blame and shame us but offers a refuge of protection and safety as he blankets us with His love.

Maintenance

Just as our homes need regular maintenance, we too need to keep ourselves in good health, bodily, mentally, and spiritually. The Bible is our instruction manual for right living. Some things we do daily and others periodically.

Every morning when we wake up, we should posture ourselves towards God and invite Him into our day. Matt. 6:33 (NIV) reads, "But seek first His Kingdom and His righteousness, and all these things will be given to you as well." Jesus is *Emmanuel*, God with us, yet so often we barely acknowledge His presence. Imagine waking up and ignoring your spouse, only remembering to talk to them when you need something.

God wants to be with us throughout the day. In Luke 18:1 Jesus told His disciples that they should always pray and not give up. He, himself, was always seeking to escape from the crowds to find time alone with God. Even if we just call on His name or thank Him, we are acknowledging Him.

We should also keep our hearts right with God so at the end of each day we can ask the Holy Spirit to check our hearts and make sure when we go to bed at night that we are not angry, offended, or unforgiving towards anyone. If we are, we can repent with sincere hearts and receive His forgiveness.

"In your anger do not sin: Do not let the sun go down while you are still angry, and do not give the devil a foothold."
(Ephesians 4:26 NIV)

Paul is not telling us never to be angry but not to let it have a hold over us.

Daily also look at your heart towards yourself.

"The second most important commandment is like this one. And it is, "Love others as much as you love yourself."
(Matthew 22:39 CEV)

Have you been harsh towards yourself today? After repenting for any wrong thoughts or actions, have you received God's forgiveness, have you forgiven yourself? Can you truly say that you love yourself? If not, you may need to spend some time with the Lord in the other rooms of the house.

Just as we need physical nourishment daily, we also need spiritual food, by reading the word and spending time talking to God. This builds our faith and renews our mind.

We should also ensure that we have times of rest and relaxation, have fun, and enjoy life. When God created the heavens and the Earth, He rested from all His work on the seventh day and He also instructed the Israelites to observe the sabbath day (from the Hebrew word, *to rest*) once a week.

We are no longer under the law, but Christians have traditionally observed one day a week, usually Sundays, to rest and worship. Whether we choose a set day or not, it is important to rest from our work to regain energy and strength. It allows us to quiet ourselves before the Lord and revive our bodies, minds, and spirits.

Every now and then we need to have a spring clean; a self-inventory to ask the Lord if there are activities or relationships in our lives that are not healthy. We also have seasons when He is working actively in healing our hearts. We should not despise these times but let him do His work As He helps get our house in order. We are the temple of the Holy Spirit.

On the Go

Wherever we go we can be sure God goes with us. Jesus lives in us and we carry the Kingdom within.

"Do you not realise about yourselves that Jesus Christ is in you."
(2 Corinthians 13:5 ESV)

We can pray at anytime, anywhere. As believers, God is dwelling in us through the Holy Spirit. We are the living temple where God resides. One day, He will come down to earth and make His dwelling place among us for all eternity.

And I heard a loud voice from the throne saying,
"Look! God's dwelling place is now among the people, and
he will dwell with them. They will be his people, and God himself
will be with them and be their God". Revelation 21:3 (NIV)

Chapter 22
PRACTICAL TOOLS

Letter Templates

As I wrote this book, I wanted to be able to tell my younger self how much God sees, hears and understands her, that He knows her and has such wonderful plans for her life. He is always with her and wants to help her on the journey.

I also wanted to encourage her to communicate with God for herself through journaling and letter writing. Remember, God is Emmanuel, which means 'God with us', and He desires to have unbroken fellowship with us. We can learn to recognise Him speaking to us for Jesus said, that His sheep know His voice.

So I have suggested a few ideas for interactive letters or conversations. At the end of the book, you can scan a QR code to my Facebook page where you will have access to more tools for engaging with God.

Prompts for Writing or Prayer

- Imagine that Father God is writing to you and telling you how He loves you and sharing the good plans He has for you.

- Your reply to Him: Be honest. Share your heart, your longings, your unhealed hurts, and unmet needs. Nothing surprises Him. He knows it all and He cares. You might want to write a letter back to yourself with His response.

- To your younger self: telling her how proud you are of her, to encourage her to be bold and courageous as you see her as God does and to help her as you know what lies ahead.

- To your own mother or daughter: in forgiveness, repentance and/or reconciliation, dealing with regrets.

- To you now: Tell yourself all the things you are proud of about yourself, and though you may not have reached your destination, you are on your way.

Exercise on Identity

As we have been discovering in this book, our identity should not come from what we do or how others define us, but from God. When Jesus asks His disciple, Peter, who he thinks Jesus is, He commends Peter as he gets the answer from His heavenly Father:

> ***"'But what about you?' he asked. 'Who do you say I am?'***
> ***Simon Peter answered, 'You are the Christ, the Son of the living God.'***
> ***Jesus replied, 'Blessed are you, Simon son of Jonah, for this was***
> ***not revealed to you by man, but by my Father in heaven.'"***
> ***(Matthew 16:15-17 NIV)***

If you remember, Jesus also told me to ask Him who he said I was; He answered that I am His beloved.

Why don't you spend some time with Jesus and ask Him:

Jesus, whose voices have I been listening to about my identity?

The devil is the accuser, but Jesus' voice is always loving and affirming. When we start to hear God correctly, we start to see ourselves correctly. His sheep know His voice and do not follow any other.

What identity or labels have people given me (including how I have seen myself) that do not represent who I am?

Jesus, who do you say I am?

Asking Jesus who you are is not a one-time question. You can bring situations to Him and ask Him what He says about you. For example, when you are feeling fearful or unlovable, ask Him what He says about you, and what is the truth? He may also want to show you different facets of your identity at different times of your life. Just as He has many names and is multi-faceted, so are you. He may want to bring out another quality you have for a particular season.

Start to develop your identity statement by writing down who Jesus says you are. You could begin with generic promises from the Bible, such as I am loved, I am known, and I am blessed. Then you can go on to what makes you unique. Speak them out and build yourself up.

YOU ARE WHO GOD SAYS YOU ARE

You are Created with a Purpose
Jeremiah 29:11

You are Beautiful
Psalm 45:11

You are Unique
Psalm 139:13

You are Loved
Jeremiah 31:3

You are Special
Ephesians 2:10

You are Cared For
Ephesians 3:17,18,19

You are Lovely
Daniel 12:3

You are Precious
1 Corinthians 6:20

You are Strong
Psalm 18:35

You are Important
1 Peter 2:9

You are Forgiven
Psalm 103:12

You are a New Creation
2 Corinthains 5:17

You are Protected
Psalm 121:3

You are Empowered
Philipians 4:13

You are Chosen
John 15:16

You are Family
Ephesians 2:19

You are Mine
Isiaih 43:1

PRESENT DAY

I am still on the journey!

Excerpt from my personal journal:

This morning I'm part way through writing my book and I'm in turmoil! I wonder how I'm ever going to finish it and help bring healing to others through it when I myself still need so much more heart healing. I go from mountain highs to valley lows. I am tossed and turned. I get to a place where I'm joyous or on an even keel and think I've made it but then plummet into hopelessness, anxiety, and self-condemnation again. When I'm like this I know all God's promises in my head and yet I don't think they're for me and believe that God is angry with me. I play over in my mind how I should have behaved better or reacted differently. I'm going to do the devil out of a job as I accuse myself! At these times I think I understand how King Saul must have felt when he was tormented by demons and needed David to play sweet soothing music to settle and calm his tormented soul. How did I get back here again? One step forward, then what seems like three steps back! It's like being in a dance where one sequence is always on repeat.

It always comes back to the treadmill of performance I have lived on for so long. When I fail on that treadmill, I believe the accuser's arrows which tell me I am a failure or a bad person. Even after saying sorry to God, I am tormented by feelings of unworthiness. In such times I must remember that He is the Lord of the Dance. He has choreographed the beginning and the end and He is dancing with me, guiding my every step; His hand in the small of my back just like Dad used to do with me as a little girl as we twirled around the sitting room. When I was very little I would stand on his feet and cling to his waist. Papa God, I cling to you in my moments of despair and self-destruction.

Very recently, following the frustration above, I had a heart healing session and the Lord pulled down a stronghold, a lie that I believed, that I am not worthy. He showed me that only He is righteous and that He is MY righteousness, *Jehovah Tsidkenhu.* There is nothing I can do to earn His approval and His banner over me is unconditional love.

There are seasons in our lives when we need to hear and experience God's love and truth again and again until it becomes our reality. The strongholds (reasonings and beliefs) in our minds can be so deeply embedded that it takes time to pull them out, just like a weed with a thick deep root. Each time the Holy Spirit revealed to me that God has made me righteous through

Jesus and that He loves me and never accuses me, the stronghold was loosened like the weed being gently loosened in the soil until finally it was ready to be pulled out. He is the master gardener so we need to trust Him and His timing.

Many times, I have been like a ship without anchor tossed about at sea, but always moving forward on its pre-ordained course. Jesus is my anchor and my destination and He knows what's best for me. Yes, He could have delivered me all at once from my fears, insecurities, and imperfections, but He knows the best way, just like the seedling in the sand that needed to be slowly nurtured and watered.

Perhaps you find it hard to identify with a ship at sea. It wasn't that long ago that people had to travel many weeks by boat to get from one continent to another, unlike our fast-paced world where aeroplanes can get us to our destination within hours. Travelling from England to Africa via the equator would have taken them from a temperate to a tropical climate over several weeks, so that by the time they got to their destination, they were acclimatized to the heat and change in humidity. Nowadays we just hop on an air-conditioned aeroplane and arrive a few hours later to the shock of a vastly different climate. As a child I remember stepping off the plane as we landed in Lagos, Nigeria and being hit by a wall of heat so I could hardly breathe. This shock to the system is not what God wants for us. His ways are gentle and kind and He often chooses the long route for us.

I share this with you to encourage you not to give up. God will complete the good work He has begun in you. He is the Alpha and Omega, the beginning and the end, the author and finisher of your faith.

My hope is this book has set you on a journey or altered your course if you have been off track; to find your identity, not as the world sees you but who God created you to be and that you will stay the course.

If you have not done so, as you journeyed with me, I encourage you to look at your own past with the help of Jesus, to see how you can rewrite the script and make course corrections as you find healing, especially from mother wounds, that brings you to accept and love yourself just as you are. To know that you are fully loved and accepted and that there is a unique and wonderful plan for your life–whatever your age. This is not to wallow in the pain of your past but to unlock doors to set you free in order to move forward.

In Jewish culture the new day begins at sunset of the previous day, so as you bring closure to the past, you too can look forward to a new dawn.

"For I am about to do something new. See, I have already begun!
Do you not see it? I will make a pathway through the wilderness.
I will create rivers in the dry wasteland."
(Isaiah 43:19 NLT)

STAY CONNECTED TO THE AUTHOR

If you have read this book and want to find out more about the book and discover resources to help you on your own journey, please go to my Facebook page

Scan
to Stay
Connected

AFTERWORD

I'm in my fifties and am visualising myself sitting on a rock along the seashore. I see a mature, older woman and as I watch her, she transforms reverting to middle age, then her younger self, a little girl, a baby, and finally an idea born in the imagination of the Father and Son. At each stage of her life the Lord tells her, "You are loved, Vanessa."

In the vision, I have a strong inner desire to show other women how beautiful and strong they are; from the old woman to the little child, to let them know they are loved at every stage of their lives and to invite them to behold Jesus as in a mirror. As they look at Him, they see their own worth and beauty and have no shame. Naked, but unashamed, perfected and ready to be His bride, accepting with joy the fullness of who He has created them to be and the destiny He has planned for them from the beginning.

"Let us rejoice and be glad and give him glory! For the wedding of the Lamb has come, and his bride has made herself ready." (Revelation 19:7 NIV)

The very last word must go to Jesus, who said this to me through a dear friend who has experienced so much pain and loss in her own life, yet always exudes love and joy, and now He says it to you. "Thank you for letting me love you."

PSALM 139

God, investigate my life; get all the facts firsthand. I'm an open book to you; even from a distance, you know what I'm thinking. You know when I leave and when I get back; I'm never out of your sight. You know everything I'm going to say before I start the first sentence. I look behind me and you're there, then up ahead and you're there, too your reassuring presence, coming and going. This is too much, too wonderful - I can't take it all in! Is there any place I can go to avoid your Spirit? to be out of your sight? If I climb to the sky, you're there! If I go underground, you're there! If I flew on morning's wings to the far western horizon, You'd find me in a minute - you're already there waiting! Then I said to myself, "Oh, he even sees me in the dark! At night I'm immersed in the light!" It's a fact: darkness isn't dark to you; night and day, darkness, and light, they're all the same to you. Oh yes, you shaped me first inside, then out; you formed me in my mother's womb. I thank you, High God - you're breathtaking! Body and soul, I am marvelously made! I worship in adoration - what a creation! You know me inside and out, you know every bone in my body; You know exactly how I was made, bit by bit, how I was sculpted from nothing into something Like an open book, you watched me grow from conception to birth all the stages of my life were spread out before you, The days of my life all prepared before I'd even lived one day. Your thoughts - how rare, how beautiful! God, I'll never comprehend them! I couldn't even begin to count them - any more than I could count the sand of the sea. Oh, let me rise in the morning and live always with you! And please, God, do away with wickedness for good! And you murderers - out of here! all the men and women who belittle you, God, infatuated with cheap god-imitations. See how I hate those who hate you, God, see how I loathe all this godless arrogance; I hate it with pure, unadulterated hatred. Your enemies are my enemies! Investigate my life, O God, find out everything about me; Cross-examine and test me, get a clear picture of what I'm about; See for yourself whether I've done anything wrong -then guide me on the road to eternal life.

REFERENCES

Pedro Adao, 100x Academy

Dan Mccollum, Bethel School of the Prophets

Bob Lonac https://www.boblonac.com/

"A Mother's Role in Early Childhood Development." Healthway Medical, 17 Apr. 2020, https://www.healthwaymedical.com/a-mothers-role-in-early-childhood-development

"Ancient Jewish Wedding Customs and Yeshua's Second Coming" Messianic Bible, 27 Apr. 2022, https://www.free.messianicbible.com/feature/ancient-jewish-wedding-customs-and-yeshuas-second-coming/

Davidson, Mark. Becoming the Beloved: The End-Time Bride of Christ. Shulamite Ministries, Publishing, 2010.

Hillsong Worship. "I Am Who You Say I Am." Hillsong Music Publishing Australia.

McClain-Walters, Michelle. The Deborah Anointing: Embracing the Call to Be a Woman of Wisdom and Discernment. Charisma House, 2015.

Michell, Roger, director. Notting Hill. Universal Pictures, 1999.

Wright, Liz, and Gretchen Rodriguez, Loved: A 90 Day Journey into the Heart of God, Liz Wright Ministries Ltd., 2021.

Zadai, Kevin L. "Warrior Notes Volume 1" Awakening

Printed in Great Britain
by Amazon